MOBILE TESTING

BCS, THE CHARTERED INSTITUTE FOR IT

BCS, The Chartered Institute for IT, is committed to making IT good for society. We use the power of our network to bring about positive, tangible change. We champion the global IT profession and the interests of individuals, engaged in that profession, for the benefit of all.

Exchanging IT expertise and knowledge

The Institute fosters links between experts from industry, academia and business to promote new thinking, education and knowledge sharing.

Supporting practitioners

Through continuing professional development and a series of respected IT qualifications, the Institute seeks to promote professional practice tuned to the demands of business. It provides practical support and information services to its members and volunteer communities around the world.

Setting standards and frameworks

The Institute collaborates with government, industry and relevant bodies to establish good working practices, codes of conduct, skills frameworks and common standards. It also offers a range of consultancy services to employers to help them adopt best practice.

Become a member

Over 70,000 people including students, teachers, professionals and practitioners enjoy the benefits of BCS membership. These include access to an international community, invitations to roster of local and national events, career development tools and a quarterly thought-leadership magazine. Visit www.bcs.org/membership to find out more.

Further Information
BCS, The Chartered Institute for IT,
First Floor, Block D,
North Star House, North Star Avenue,
Swindon, SN2 1FA, United Kingdom.
T +44 (0) 1793 417 424
F +44 (0) 1793 417 444
(Monday to Friday, 09:00 to 17:00 UK time)
www.bcs.org/contact

http://shop.bcs.org/

MOBILE TESTING
An ASTQB-BCS foundation guide

Rex Black

Published by BCS Learning & Development Ltd, a wholly owned subsidiary of BCS, The Chartered Institute for IT, First Floor, Block D, North Star House, North Star Avenue, Swindon, SN2 1FA, UK.
www.bcs.org

Paperback ISBN: 978-1-78017-404-4
PDF ISBN: 978-1-78017-405-1
ePUB ISBN: 978-1-78017-406-8
Kindle ISBN: 978-1-78017-407-5

British Cataloguing in Publication Data.
A CIP catalogue record for this book is available at the British Library.

BCS books are available at special quantity discounts to use as premiums and sale promotions, or for use in corporate training programmes. Please visit our Contact us page at www.bcs.org/contact

Publisher's acknowledgements
Reviewer: Piotr Wicherski, Gary Rueda, Dawn Haynes and JeanAnn Harrison
Publisher: Ian Borthwick
Commissioning Editor: Rebecca Youé
Production Manager: Florence Leroy
Project Manager: Sunrise Setting Ltd
Cover work: Alex Wright
Picture credits: Belish/Shutterstock

Typeset by Lapiz Digital Services, Chennai, India.

CONTENTS

LIST OF FIGURES AND TABLES

FIGURES

TABLES

ABOUT THE AUTHOR

Rex Black has over 30 years of software and systems engineering experience. He is the President of RBCS (www.rbcs-us.com), a leader in software, hardware, and systems testing. For almost 25 years, RBCS has delivered consulting, training and expert services for software, hardware, and systems testing and quality. Employing the industry's most experienced and recognized consultants, RBCS builds and improves testing groups and provides testing experts for hundreds of clients worldwide. Ranging from Fortune 20 companies to start-ups, RBCS clients save time and money through higher quality, reduced risk of production failures, improved product development, improved reputation, and more.

Rex has authored over a dozen training courses, many of them ISTQB® accredited. These materials have been used to train tens of thousands of people internationally, both directly through RBCS on-site, virtual, public, and e-learning courses as well as through a worldwide network of licensed training partners in Europe, Africa, the United States, Latin America, the Middle East, Australasia, East Asia, and Southern Asia. In addition to for-profit training courses, Rex has presented an hour-long, monthly, free webinar for over seven years; this webinar series has reached over 40,000 registrants. Rex has written over 50 articles, presented hundreds of papers, workshops, webinars, and seminars, and given over a hundred keynotes and other speeches at conferences and events around the world.

Rex is the past President of the International Software Testing Qualifications Board and of the American Software Testing Qualifications Board. He holds a Bachelor's of Science degree in Computer Science and Engineering from the University of California, Los Angeles (UCLA) and a Master's Certificate in Software Testing from Villanova University.

Rex is the most prolific author practicing in the field of software testing today. His popular first book, *Managing the Testing Process*, has sold over 100,000 copies around the world, including Japanese, Chinese, and Indian releases, and is now in its third edition. His other books on testing, *Agile Testing Foundations*, *Advanced Software Testing: Volumes I, II, and III*, *Critical Testing Processes*, *Foundations of Software Testing*, *Pragmatic Software Testing*, *Fundamentos de Pruebas de Software*, *Testing Metrics*, *Improving the Testing Process*, *Improving the Software Process*, and *The Expert Test Manager* have also sold tens of thousands of copies, including Spanish, Chinese, Japanese, Hebrew, Hungarian, Indian, and Russian editions.

You can find Rex on Twitter (@RBCS), on Facebook (@TestingImprovedbyRBCS), on LinkedIn (rex-black), and on YouTube (RBCSINC).

ACKNOWLEDGEMENTS

This book grew out of an accredited training course, based on a syllabus developed by the American Software Testing Qualifications Board (ASTQB). I'd like to thank my RBCS colleagues Jared Pauletti and Dena Pauletti for their help with the course that became this book. I'd also like to thank the reviewers, JeanAnn Harrison, Dawn Haynes, and Gary Rueda Sandoval, for their useful input on the draft chapters of this book.

Finally, a big thank you to my wife, Laurel Becker, my children, Emma and Charlotte, and our canine pack, Kibo, Mmink, and Roscoe, for always being there, even when the times get tough.

GLOSSARY

All definitions are taken, with permission, from the ASTQB[1] Mobile Tester Glossary.

Emulator   A device, computer program or system that accepts the same inputs and produces the same outputs as a given system.

Geolocation   The identification of the real-world geographical location of a device.

Hybrid application   A mobile application that requires communication with the web server but also utilizes plug-ins to access device functionality.

Minimal essential test strategy   A lightweight approach to risk analysis sometimes used when testing mobile applications. Acronym: METS.

Mobile application testing   Testing that is conducted on mobile applications.

Mobile web application   A mobile application that is designed for use by a variety of devices with the majority of the code residing on the web server.

Native device   The actual physical device that is running a mobile application.

Native mobile application   A mobile application that is designed for a specific device family and is coded to access specific functionality of the device normally via tools that have been specifically designed for the device.

Operational profile   The representation of a distinct set of tasks performed by the component or system, possibly based on user behaviour when interacting with the component or system, and their probabilities of occurrence. A task is logical rather than physical and can be executed over several machines or be executed in non-contiguous time segments.

Risk analysis   The process of assessing identified project or product risks to determine their level of risk, typically by estimating their impact and probability of occurrence (likelihood).

Simulator   A device, computer program or system used during testing, which behaves or operates like a given system when provided with a set of controlled inputs.

TestStorming   A technique used to derive test cases using techniques such as brainstorming or mind maps.

---

[1] Available here: https://certifications.bcs.org/upload/pdf/swt-foundation-mobile-tester-glossary.pdf

INTRODUCTION

"I think there is a world market for maybe five computers." So said Thomas Watson, president of IBM, in 1943.

Back in the 1960s, when I was born, we already had way more than five computers. We even had spacecraft that went to the moon with computers on them, so we already had mobile computing devices. However, the Apollo Guidance Computer had 4 KB RAM, 72 KB of read-only storage, and a 2 MHz, 16-bit, single-core CPU. My current phone has 3 GB RAM, 32 GB of built-in storage and 128 GB SD storage, and a 1.8 GHz, 64-bit, six-core CPU. Back in the 1960s, we already had mobile phones, too, but they had to be installed in cars, because they relied on lead-acid batteries and drew 250 watts.

The marriage of mobile computing and mobile phones started in the 1990s, with the Simon Personal Communicator, the first phone with a touchscreen, email, calendar, contact management, and even the ability to add apps. Ironically enough, given Watson's comments 50 years earlier, this was an IBM product. Fifty thousand sold. So, Watson's prediction was off by four orders of magnitude just in terms of smartphones within 50 years.

In 2014, according an article in *The Independent*, the number of mobile devices officially passed the number of human beings. So, 70 years after Watson's prediction, he's already off by nine orders of magnitude.[1]

The growth of devices is not the only amazing growth rate associated with mobile devices and their apps. The number of mobile apps continues to grow rapidly, and the number of hours spent using mobile apps per day is growing at an exponential rate. Mobile apps are being used for everything from entertainment to business networking to law enforcement to health-care management.

So, mobile devices and their apps are clearly on a stunning, transformative path. However, as mobile devices and their apps become more and more embedded in our lives, the consequences of failures goes up. From frustrations with slow, balky, or hard-to-understand apps to people being killed or injured, the stakes get higher and higher. At the same time, the expectations of users and managers, along with the pressures of a super-competitive environment, push for more and more functionality, faster and faster. In addition to all the things that usually make testing challenging, these opposing

---

[1] You can find the referenced article online at: www.independent.co.uk/life-style/gadgets-and-tech/news/there-are-officially-more-mobile-devices-than-people-in-the-world-9780518.html

forces—high risks associated with poor quality versus a fanatical speed-to-market imperative—create huge additional challenges for us as test professionals.

So, if you are testing mobile apps, and finding yourself confronted with huge testing challenges, this book is for you. I don't pretend to have all the answers—far from it—but I do hope to provide you with some answers and some good hints on how to find even more answers. The exercises, along with their solutions, will help you think through some of the challenges.

In addition, if you are looking to study for the ASTQB Certified Mobile Tester exam,[2] this book will provide a handy study guide for you. It covers the entire syllabus and includes study questions. Combine this book with an accredited training course (such as the RBCS Mobile Tester Foundation course), the syllabus itself and the sample exams you can download, and you should be well prepared.

Whether your objectives are work-related, certification-related, or both, I hope you enjoy this book, and find it a useful companion. Send me your feedback via your favorite social media app, running on your favorite mobile device. I look forward to hearing from you.

BOOK STYLE

You'll notice that in each chapter I've included a list of terms to remember. You can check the definitions of these terms in the ASTQB and ISTQB® glossaries.

To be clear with respect to these terms, it is possible that you will get questions in the Mobile Tester exam that have to do with their definitions. It might be a question that simply asks, "What is the Internet of Things?" In that case, the correct answer matches the definition of the Internet of Things. However, it might be a question that asks about the application of a testing technique, but, to select the right answer, you also have to know the difference between a hybrid application, a native mobile application, and a mobile web application. So, you will need to study the definitions of the terms as part of preparing for the exam.

A note on learning objectives and knowledge levels

At the beginning of each section, you're going to see learning objectives or LOs'. Each of those LOs has what is called a K level or knowledge level. What are learning objectives and knowledge levels?

The pedantic definition and use of a learning objective is to measure and quantify—to the extent possible—what and how deeply one should learn from a training course or book on the topic, and what and how profoundly one should know a particular topic to pass the exam. The ISTQB® 2018 and the ASTQB have adopted this concept for their syllabi, in part to ensure consistency of exams around the world and also to aid in achieving consistent training courses.

---

[2] See https://certifications.bcs.org/category/18802

So, the Mobile Testing Foundation exam is based on learning objectives, and the same learning objectives underpin this book. We'll introduce the learning objectives for each section at the beginning of that section.

The learning objectives are at four levels of increasing sophistication:

- K1: remember basic facts, techniques, and standards;
- K2: understand the facts, techniques, and standards and how they inter-relate;
- K3: apply facts, techniques, and standards to your projects;
- K4: analyze a scenario to determine which facts, techniques, and standards apply to the scenario.

Let me explain the difference between these K levels with some examples. First, let's look at the difference between K1 and K2. Obviously, in order to understand something, you'd have to remember it. However, understanding is a higher level of knowledge than remembering. As an example, I went to UCLA and got an engineering degree there. Part of that degree program was a two-year-long, six-class series of math classes. It started with basic calculus, derivatives, and integrals. It culminated in a class on matrix mathematics and related topics.

I really hated that class. I still sometimes have a nightmare that I'm going to my final for that class, with visions of matrices and eigenvalues and matrix inversions and so forth swimming around in my head. In my nightmare, and in my real life now, I remember what those are, but don't understand them. So, I have K1 knowledge of matrix mathematics left over from that class, but no K2 or K3 knowledge, which I had (just barely) at the time of the final. In real life, I remember walking out of the final, thinking, "Thank God that's the last in that series of math classes, because if there were one more level of difficulty beyond that, I would not be able to be an engineer."

Now, let's look at the difference between K2 and K3. Again, obviously, you can't apply a technique without actually understanding it, but just because you understand something doesn't meant that you can apply it. As an example, similar to the two-year-long series of math classes, we also had a two-year series of physics classes. One that I remember particularly well covered topics like harmonics, how springs work, how musical instruments work and so forth.

I found those topics fascinating for some reason, and the material has stuck with me to some extent over these years. I can explain to you how a piano or a violin works. However, can I calculate the harmonic frequency of a guitar string? No. I have K1 and K2 knowledge of how musical instruments work, but I have no practical ability to apply that knowledge to do anything; that is, I have no remaining K3 knowledge.

In terms of the difference between K3 and K4, in a K3 situation, you must be able to apply your knowledge, but you are told in advance what knowledge is required. In a K4 situation, you must determine what knowledge is required first. For example, if you tell me that you have a table with numbers showing the velocity of an object over a period of time, and you need to determine its rate of acceleration, then I would know how to set up a table in a spreadsheet to get an equation for the velocity, and then use differentiation (differential calculus) to find the acceleration, because I still have K4 knowledge of basic calculus stuck in my head.

What kind of exam questions can you expect? Different exam and national boards can have somewhat different exams. However, the following rules of thumb should hold for most exams.

The entire Mobile Tester Foundation syllabus is implicitly covered at the K1 level, which means that K1 knowledge of the syllabus can be necessary to get the right answer for any question in the exam, though the question may also require K2, K3, or K4 knowledge as well. There are 40 questions in the exam. Approximately speaking, 25 percent of those questions are K1 questions, 50 percent are K2 questions, 25 percent are K3 questions, and there is a single K4 question. Like the Foundation exam and unlike the Advanced exams, regardless of K level, each question is worth one point. You will need 65 percent to pass the exam, which might seem easy, but the questions can be hard.

While the ISTQB® Foundation syllabus 2018 is not directly examinable, there will be questions that relate to material covered in that syllabus. Therefore, I strongly recommend reviewing the ISTQB® Foundation syllabus 2018.[3]

---

[3] You can find the Foundation syllabus here: www.istqb.org/downloads/syllabi/foundation-level-syllabus.html

1   INTRODUCTION TO MOBILE TESTING

In this chapter, we'll lay the ground for the material to come in this book. We'll start by talking about mobile devices, which are the platforms on which mobile apps run, and then about different types of mobile apps. Next, we'll look at what mobile users expect from their devices and the apps running on them. This will bring us to the topic of how these mobile device and app realities, along with the expectations of the users, create challenges for testers, which will introduce a core set of topics for the subsequent chapters. We will also introduce the topic of tester skills for mobile testing, and then equipment requirements, both of which are topics we'll return to later in the book. Finally, we'll briefly look at software development life cycle models and how the ongoing changes in the way software is built are influencing model app development.

This book is not about software testing in general, but about mobile app testing in particular. So, while this chapter does not delve into the details of how mobile app testing differs from software testing in general, each of the subsequent chapters will explore those differences in detail.

CHAPTER SECTIONS

Chapter 1, Introduction to Mobile Testing, contains the following six sections:

1. What is a mobile application?
2. Expectations from mobile users
3. Challenges for testers
4. Necessary skills
5. Equipment requirements
6. Life cycle models

CHAPTER TERMS

The terms to remember for Chapter 1 are as follows:

- hybrid application;
- Internet of Things;
- mobile application testing;

- mobile web application;
- native mobile application;
- wearables testing.

1 WHAT IS A MOBILE APPLICATION?

The learning objective for Chapter 1, Section 1, is recall of syllabus content only.

First, let's look at what a mobile device is. There are two types of mobile device—general purpose mobile devices and purpose-built devices, either mass market or proprietary. Purpose-built devices are built for a specific purpose or set of purposes. A smart watch is an example. Another example is the e-reader, though these are evolving away from purpose built to general purpose—consider Kindles. The newer Kindles are more like a fully-fledged tablet now than the original Kindles.

Proprietary purpose-built devices include the package tracking and signature devices used by various delivery services around the world. When you receive a package, you sign on the device itself. Once you've signed on that, you can go to the appropriate website, which will show that the package was delivered. Behind the scenes, the mobile device communicated to a server. That information in turn propagated to the delivery company's online website. A pretty complex data flow happens in the process of doing something that appears to be fairly mundane: acknowledging receipt of a package.

Keep in mind that if you are testing a purpose-built mobile device or an application for such a device, everything we're discussing will be applicable, plus whatever is specific and unique about your purpose-built device and its applications.

General purpose mobile devices are those that can run various apps, downloadable from app stores such as those for Android and Apple devices; can be extended with external peripherals, such as Bluetooth headsets and keyboards; can be used for a wide (and ever-growing) variety of tasks; and have a wide (and ever-expanding) set of sensors that allow them to interact with the physical world in ways that set mobile devices apart from the typical PC. Examples include smartphones, tablets, and netbooks.

In this book, we will focus mostly on general purpose mobile devices and the applications that run on them. We won't talk much about "dumb" phones, since those generally support only calls and texts, with no ability to install additional apps. So, it's unlikely that you're building apps for a dumb phone.

There are two basic types of mobile applications. One type is a native mobile app. The other type is a mobile-optimized website. (It's a little more complicated than that, but let's keep it simple for the moment.) Native mobile apps run on your mobile device directly, while mobile-optimized websites run on your mobile device's browser. Native mobile apps are downloaded from an app store and installed on your device. Mobile-optimized websites—including websites designed using responsive techniques—are simply websites that look and behave nicely on your device's browser and hardware.

Some organizations have both types of mobile apps. For example, United Airlines and Delta Airlines have apps that you can download and mobile-optimized websites that you can reach at their appropriate URLs, either united.com or delta.com. If your organization goes down this route, it increases the challenge from a testing point of view.

Let's consider how this has unfolded over time. Suppose you are involved with testing Delta's online presence. About a decade ago, there was delta.com and the website there. That was the online presence. Whether with a PC or a smartphone or an internet appliance (if you know what that was), you'd go to delta dot com and you'd see the same thing. Of course, with a smartphone, you'd see it on a smaller screen and it'd be a lot more difficult to read and navigate. Then, mobile-optimized websites came along and companies started to build apps. So now, if you are testing Delta's online presence, you have to deal with all three options: the mobile-optimized website, the normal website and the native mobile app. There are a number of things that you'd need to consider across those three different platforms. These are topics that we're going to talk about in this book, so you can recognize and deal with those related, overlapping, but nonetheless different situations.

1.1 Test your knowledge

Let's try one or more sample exam questions related to the material we've just covered. The answers are found in Appendix C.

Question 1 Learning objective: recall of syllabus content only (K1)

Which of the following statements is true?

    A. All mobile apps are general purpose.
    B. All mobile apps are portable across mobile devices.
    C. Browsers are used by all mobile apps.
    D. The number of mobile apps available grows by the day.

Question 2 Learning objective: term understanding (K1)

What is a native mobile application?

    A. A mobile application that requires communication with the web server but also utilizes plug-ins to access device functionality.
    B. A mobile application that is designed for use by a variety of devices, with the majority of the code residing on the web server.
    C. A mobile application that is designed for a specific device family and is coded to access specific functionality of the device.
    D. The actual physical device that is running a mobile application.

2 EXPECTATIONS FROM MOBILE USERS

The learning objective for Chapter 1, Section 2, is as follows:

MOB-1.2.1   (K2) Explain the expectations for a mobile application user and how this affects test prioritization.

On a typical morning or afternoon, when I'm working from my home office, you can find me in a gym, working out, and listening to a podcast on my mobile phone. I might be checking social media updates and the news while I'm doing this. As an aging gym rat, my workouts don't require a lot of focus, as it's mostly about maintaining a certain level of muscle tone and general fitness.

Often, I'm surrounded by younger folks who are still on the upward path from a health and fitness perspective, putting in serious gym time, dripping sweat on treadmills or lifting a couple hundred pounds of iron. But, when I look up from my phone, guess what? Most of the people around me are in the same position, head bent forward, looking intently at a small screen, Bluetooth headphones in their ears. Imagine how completely bizarre this scene would appear to a gym rat from the 1970s.[1]

It's not just at gyms. It's everywhere. Worldwide, there is a new public health risk to pedestrians: being struck and in some cases, killed by cars because they—and sometimes the driver—were so engrossed in the little world of their little screen that they failed to avoid an obvious hazard.

So, public health and gym culture aside, what does all this mean for you as a tester?

Well, you should assume—if you're lucky—that your users will interact with your app daily or hourly or maybe even continuously! But, before they do, you need to test it. Is it completely obvious how your app works? Does it work fast? Does it always work?

The further away your app's behavior is from those expectations—reasonable or otherwise—the bigger the problem. There are millions of mobile apps out there, often with hundreds in each category. And in each category, for any one thing you're trying to do, you're likely to be able to find different options.

So, suppose a user downloads your mobile app, and, within seconds, the user's not happy. Your app's not very reliable. Or it's too hard to figure out. Or it's really slow. Or it´s really difficult to install or configure for initial use. What does the user do? That's right: uninstall your app, download your competitor's app, and, shazam, your erstwhile user is now a former user. Oh, yeah, and a dissatisfied one, too. Here comes the one-star review on the app store.

Now, some of you reading might have a captive audience, a cadre of users who can't bail on you. For example, your company creates a mobile app that other employees use to do some certain thing. In this case, they can't just abandon it. But if these users are

---

[1] If you're having a hard time visualizing the gym scene without mobile devices, watch the Arnold Schwarzenegger movie, *Pumping Iron* (1977), that introduced the soon-to-be-movie-star, and gym culture in general, to a wider audience.

dissatisfied, now two bad things happen. First, the company bears the cost of the inefficiency, the lost time, and the mistakes. Second, employee satisfaction suffers, because people compare your pathetic in-house app to all the other cool apps they have on their phone. Eventually, these bad things come home to roost with the development team that created the hated app and inflicted it on the other employees.

I have a client that operates a chain of home improvement stores. They have both a brick-and-mortar presence and an online presence. Doing business purely online doesn't make sense, as sometimes you need a rake or a shovel or a sack of concrete right now.

Now, if you've been in a large home improvement store, you probably know that it's not always obvious where you find particular things. In addition, sometimes stuff gets sold out.

So, my client issued iPhones to all its associates, and installed a custom-built app on them. If a customer approached an associate and asked, "Where are your shovels?" the associate could say, "Shovels are in this particular aisle, this particular location."

In fact, the associate could even add, "By the way, we're sold out of square-point shovels, but we happen to have some available at our other store at such-and-such location." That was because the app was able to communicate with the back-end inventory systems. The app knew that the current store didn't have something in stock, and automatically found the nearest store that had it. Further, if the customer didn't want to drive over and get the square-point shovel, the associate could use the app to send a request that the missing shovel should be sent to their store for a pick up later.

That's some fairly sophisticated capability. If it's slow, if it's hard to figure out, if it's unreliable, then the associate will be frustrated while they're trying to solve this dilemma of the missing square-point. If it's bad enough, the customer might just walk away, muttering something like, "Nice whiz-bang technology, too bad it doesn't work." Now you're back in former customer territory again.

The scope of the mobile app challenge is only going to grow. This is a very, very rapidly evolving market. At the time I wrote this book, there were around six million mobile apps across the Android, Apple, Windows, Amazon, and Blackberry platforms. That's a huge number, and a lot of competition. Furthermore, the number seems to be equal to, or perhaps even greater than, the number of applications available for Windows, Mac, and Linux PCs.

This embarrassment of riches feeds users' unreasonably high expectations of quality and their unreasonably high expectations of how fast they'll get new features. People want all the new bells and whistles, all the new functionality. They want apps to be completely reliable. They want apps to be very fast. They want apps to be trivially easy to install, configure, and use.

With mobile apps as with anything else, as testers, we should focus our attention on the user. Try to think about testing from the users' point of view.

Let's consider an airline mobile app. Who's the target user? Typically, the frequent flyer. From the users' perspective, if you only travel every now and then, why go through the trouble of downloading and installing an app when you could just go to the mobile-optimized website? Even for those infrequent travelers who do use the app, they are not the airlines' main customers.

So, what does our target user, the frequent flyer, want to do? Well, as a frequent flyer, I often use such apps to check details on my flights. For example, is there a meal? What gate does it leave from?

When I use these apps, I'm concerned with functionality, and also usability. For example, at one point on the Delta app, it had a page called "my reservations" that would show various kinds of information about a reservation, but not whether the flight had a meal. However, you could find the meal details on the appropriate flight status page. To get there, I had to back out of "my reservations," remember (or find) the flight number, enter the flight number, and click to check the status. Then, buried in an obscure place on that page was an option to see the amenities—represented as icons rather than in words, as if to make it even less clear.

Okay, so the functionality was there, but the usability was pretty poor. The information was a good seven or eight clicks away from the "my reservation" page. Besides, there's just no good reason not to include the answer to an obvious question—are you going to feed me?

Another important feature for a frequent flyer is to be able to check weather and maps for connections and destination cities. For example, if I've got a connection, I'll want to know if there is weather in that area that might cause some inbound delays. If so, maybe I want to hedge my bets and get on a later connecting flight. If I'm arriving somewhere, I might want to quickly call up a map and see where the airport is in relationship to my hotel.

So, there's an interoperability element. The app won't have that ability embedded within itself; it calls other apps on the device. Sometimes that works, but I've had plenty of times when it didn't—at least not the first time.

There's also a portability element. I want to be able to solve my travel problems regardless of what kind of device I'm using at the time. So, whether I'm using my phone, or my tablet, or my PC, I want similar functionality and a similar way to access it.

Unfortunately, the users' desire for consistency is something that organizations seem to have a lot of trouble getting right. Obviously, there will be some user interface differences by necessity. But, just like driving a car and driving a truck feel similar enough that there's no problem moving from one to the other, the same should apply to apps, regardless of the platform. When you test different platforms—and you certainly should—make sure that your test oracles include your app on other platforms.

The problem is exacerbated by siloing in larger organizations. There can be three different groups of people developing and testing the mobile-optimized website, the native app, and the full-size website.

Going back to the frequent flyer example, I need to use these apps or mobile-optimized websites under a wide variety of circumstances. Whether I have a Wi-Fi connection, fast or slow. Whether I have only a 4G or 3G data connection. In fact, the more urgent travel problems are likely to arise in situations with challenging connectivity. For example, when you're running through an airport.

Speed and reliability can be big concerns too. If I'm in the middle of trying to solve a screwed up travel situation, the last thing I want is to watch a little spinning icon, or have to start over when the app crashes.

In addition to the users' perspective, the airline also is a stakeholder, and that perspective has to be considered when testing. For example, with international customers there could be some localization issues related to supporting different languages.

The airline wants to make it easy for a potential customer to go from looking for a particular flight on a particular day to actually purchasing a seat on the flight. If this natural use case—browse, find, purchase—is too hard, a frequent flyer can move from one airline's app to another.

Ultimately, the airline wants its app to help gain market share. It does that by solving the frequent flyers' typical problems, reliably, quickly, and easily.

Most of you probably aren't testing airline apps. However, whatever type of app you are testing, you have to do the same kind of user and stakeholder analysis I just walked you through. It's critical to consider the different, relevant quality characteristics. We'll cover this in more detail later.

So, you've now met your user—and she (or he) is you, right, or at least a lot like you? You probably interact with apps on your mobile device daily, hourly, in some cases continuously. You probably expect those apps to be self-explanatory, fast, and reliable. When you get a new app, you expect it to be easy to install and easy to learn, or you abandon it. So, when you're testing, remember to think like your user. Of course, you'll need to test in a lot of different situations, which is something we'll explore a lot more in this book.

1.2 Test your knowledge

Let's try one or more sample exam questions related to the material we've just covered. The answers are found in Appendix C.

Question 3 Learning objective: MOB-1.2.1 (K2) Explain the expectations for a mobile application user and how this affects test prioritization

Which of the following is a typical scenario involving a mobile app that does not meet user expectations for ease-of-use?

    A. Users abandon the app and find another with better usability.
    B. Users continue to use the app, as their options are limited.
    C. Users become frustrated by the app's slow performance.
    D. Testers should focus on usability for the next release.

3 CHALLENGES FOR TESTERS

The learning objectives for Chapter 1, Section 3, are as follows:

MOB-1.3.1   (K2) Explain the challenges testers encounter in mobile application testing and how the environments and skills must change to address those challenges.

MOB-1.3.2   (K2) Summarize the different types of mobile applications.

In this section, we'll take a broad look at some topics we'll cover deeply later, as well as revisiting the different types of mobile apps to add more clarity.

The number of uses for mobile apps just keeps on growing. While writing this book, for example, I checked and found that there are actually Fitbit-type devices and mobile apps for dogs—six of them. They allow you to monitor your dog's exercise levels and so forth. If you've got an overweight dog, I suppose that makes sense.

However, some mobile applications are much more mission critical or safety critical. One of our clients, in the health-care management business, manages hospitals, emergency rooms, urgent care facilities, doctors' offices, and pharmacies. This is obviously mission critical and safety critical. They have mobile apps that are used by health-care practitioners. Imagine if the app gets somebody's blood type wrong, misses a drug allergy or interaction, or something similar. A person could die.

Further, the number of people who are using mobile apps is huge. It's in excess of a billion, and it's growing.[2] Just think, a little over a decade ago, the one-laptop-per-child idea was seen as edgy and revolutionary. Now it seems almost quaint, with smartphones everywhere.

I've heard reports from relief workers that, if you go into some refugee camps, you will find people trading their food rations so they can pay their mobile phone bills. It is more essential to them to have a working phone than to eat, and there are good reasons for that apparently. The phone is their connection to the outside world, and thus is one of their few ways of leveraging their way out of those camps. It's a remarkable concept on a number of levels.

So, ranging from private jets to refugee camps to everywhere in between, mobile devices and their apps are completely ubiquitous now, yet this promises to only explode further. How? Well, the Internet of Things seems on track to gradually expand to the point where every single object has an IP address. Refrigerator, dryer, stop light, vending machine, billboard, implantable medical device, and even you. Such immersion in a sea of continuous processing, possibly with your place in it via some optimized reality beyond what the Google Glass offered, or even virtual reality, has some challenging social implications.

---

[2] As you can see on the link here, multiple apps have more than one billion users, so the total number of mobile app users must be well over one billion: www.statista.com/topics/1002/mobile-app-usage/

Just from a testing point of view, it's mind-boggling. How will we deal with all of this? This book doesn't have all the answers, but I hope to give you some ideas of how to chip away at the problems.

Software releases

One of the problems is the firehose of software releases. Release after release after release. Marketing and sales people say, "We gotta get this new feature out, and we gotta get that new feature out, jeez, our competitors just got those features out, we gotta get those new features out."

There's a fine line between speed-to-market and junk-to-market, and users will be fickle when confronted with junk. It's certainly not unusual for an insufficiently tested update to occur, causing users to howl as their favorite features break. Maybe they become former users. Maybe your app gets a lot of one-star reviews on the app store.

You can't just test the app. You also must test how the app gets on the device, the installation and the update processes. When those processes go wrong, they can cause more trouble than a few bugs in a new feature.

So, part of the solution, which I'll cover in more detail in Chapter 4, is the range of tools out there to help you cover more features and configurations in less time. Further, a lot of these are open-source tools, which is good, because free is always in budget, though you have to consider your own time working with the tool.

Further, a tool is not a magic wand. You need to have the skills to use the tool. You also need to have the time to use the tool, and the time to do sufficient testing with the tool.

Covering functional and non-functional quality characteristics

Users typically use software because it exhibits certain behaviors that they want or need. The ISTQB® has adopted the industry-standard approach of broadly classifying these characteristics as functional and non-functional. Functional characteristics have to do with *what* the software does, while non-functional characteristics have to do with *how* the software does what it does.

In testing, we need to address both functional and non-functional characteristics. For example, we have to test functionality, to see whether the software solves the right problem and gives the right answers. We also need to consider non-functional tests—if it matters whether the software solves problems quickly, reliably and securely, on all supporting hardware platforms, in a way that the users find easy to learn, easy to use, and pleasing to use. This need to address both functional and non-functional aspects of the software presents another set of challenges. Let's illustrate this challenge with an example.

Figure 1.1 shows an example of the Adler Airlines app on a Windows device.[3] We'll see a contrasting example of the Adler app on an Android device a little later, which will add yet another dimension of test coverage. If you look at this app, there are some features

---

[3] Don't bother searching online for flights from Adler Airlines. The example airline apps are entirely fictitious.

Figure 1.1 The Adler app welcome screen

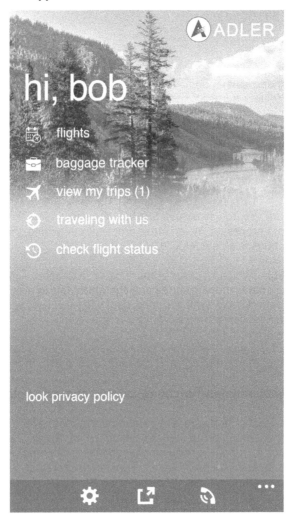

that require connectivity, such as checking flight status. Some features do not, such as looking at existing trips that have already been downloaded to the phone.

For the features that don't require connectivity, you can test those in a test lab or cubicle or wherever. However, for features that do require connectivity, consider this: if you're sitting in a test lab with stable and strong Wi-Fi and cellular signals, is that a good simulation of the users' experience? In addition, you must consider different devices, different amounts of memory, different amounts of storage, different screen sizes, and so forth.

In addition to portability and connectivity, is security an issue for this app? Performance? Reliability? Usability? Yes, probably all of the above.

If you look closely at the screen, you can see there're quite a few features here. For example, under the "traveling with us" selection, there are a bunch of specific features, such as being able to find Adler's airline clubs. So, with each new release, there's a bunch of functionality that needs regression testing.

There's often more than one

Keep in mind, the user is just trying to solve a problem. The native apps (for however many platforms), the mobile-optimized website, the website as seen on a PC browser: for the user, these are just tools, a means to an end. The user wants to grab a device, whatever happens to be handy, whatever happens to enable them to get a connection at that moment, and solve their problem. They want to be able to solve the problem quickly, easily, whichever device they use. Further, a user might use one device and then come back and use another device to continue work.

For example, if the user books a flight using the native app, then goes to the airline's website on their PC, the user expects to immediately see that reservation. This is true whether both access methods query the same database or whether there is a different back-end database for each. In other words, data synchronization and migration are critical, across all of the intended target devices here. You'll need to consider portability across those devices. Whichever device users grab, they'll expect the user interface to be consistent enough that the cross-platform user experience is, at least, not disconcerting and frustrating.

It's not that the users don't like you, but they are unlikely to be sympathetic to the significant increase in testing complexity that's created by the fact that you've got three very distinct ways of getting at the same functionality. In fact, there might be two or three distinct native apps (one for each major phone operating system) that need testing, plus you have to test the websites on multiple browsers. Most users don't know about that and probably wouldn't care. They want it all to work, and they want new features all the time, and, if you do break something, they want bug fixes right away—because that's the expectation that's been created by all the options out there.

As I mentioned before, in the case of enterprise applications, you might have less of a problem. For example, my client in the home improvement store business standardized on the iPhone, in a particular configuration. However, the trend is towards enterprises allowing what's called BYOD—bring your own device—so you'd be back in the same scenario in terms of testing supported devices.

So, it's almost certain that you're facing a real challenge with testing supported configurations. We'll address ways to handle these challenges in great detail later in this book. For the moment, though, let me point out that the type of app you're dealing with matters quite a bit, especially in terms of test strategy and risk.

If your company is still in the mobile device dark ages, you might only have to test a single website, designed for PC browsers. That might work functionally, and it makes your life a lot easier, but it probably looks horrible on a small screen and makes the user unhappy. Maybe you have a mobile-optimized website. As I mentioned before, this can be a separate site or it can be the same site based on responsive web design technology.

In either case, these can be classic thin-client implementations. There's no code running on the mobile device, other than the browsers. That makes testing easier, because portability is down to one or two browsers on each supported mobile device. However, you can't take advantage of any of the capabilities of the mobile device, other than those the browser can access, such as location.

So, your development team might decide to go with a thicker-client approach. This involves creating plug-ins for the browser that can access device features. This is obviously easier from a development point of view, but, for testing, you start to get into the portability challenges of a native app. Further, you might not get the same abilities to work disconnected as a native app would provide.

Moving further along the road toward a native mobile app are the hybrid mobile apps. These have some elements of a web-based app but also some native elements that provide access to device features. Depending on the native elements and the features accessed, you could have almost all the portability challenges of a native app. You'll need to test every device feature used by the native code. However, developers can build a fully-functioned mobile app more quickly, since they enjoy some of the benefits of web-based development.

Once you get into having one or more native mobile apps, you've really entered the supported configurations testing morass. There are a huge number of possibilities. It's likely that you'll have to resort to some mix of actual hardware—yours and other people's—and simulators. We'll discuss this further in Chapter 4.

Let's look more closely at the Adler mobile app and the Adler mobile website. In Figure 1.2, you see the Adler mobile app running on an Android phone. In Figure 1.3, you see the mobile-optimized Adler website.

The features are more or less the same, which is what the user would want. The user interface is different, but moving between them isn't too challenging. However, the code is different. So, there are now two opportunities for a particular bug in a particular feature.

In addition, the distribution of work between the client-side and the server-side is different between the two. The native app can do more on the client-side, while the mobile-optimized website must rely more on the server-side. For example, I can do things on the native app that on the mobile-optimized website appear to be done on my phone, but they're actually done on the server. I can use the native app without a connection. Certain features, like checking flight status, don't work offline, but many features do work. Now, I can't use the mobile-optimized website without a connection. Even if I have the webpage loaded in my browser, if I try to do anything on it and don't have a connection, I'll get an error message.

Figure 1.2 The Adler mobile app

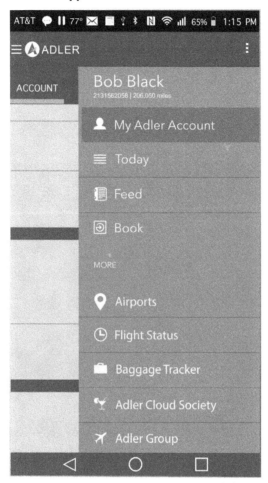

So I have basically the same features, albeit with a somewhat different user interface and very different behavior if there's no connection. The user can use either to achieve their travel goal, but for us as testers they are distinct, different things. Each must be tested, and tested in ways that address the risks to system quality posed by each.

1.3 Test your knowledge

Let's try one or more sample exam questions related to the material we've just covered. The answers are found in Appendix C.

Figure 1.3 The Adler mobile website

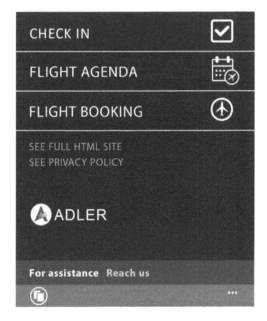

Question 4 Learning objective: MOB-1.3.1 (K2) Explain the challenges testers encounter in mobile application testing and how the environments and skills must change to address those challenges

Which of the following statements is true?

    A. The set of mobile apps is limited by the cost of integrated development environments.

    B. The set of devices supported by any given mobile app can be limited by the cost of test environments.

    C. There is usually enough time for testing at the end of each release cycle.

    D. Testing can be focused on a single device/browser combination, due to similarities in behavior.

Question 5 Learning objective: MOB-1.3.2 (K2) Summarize the different types of mobile applications

A mobile app runs entirely on a server, with no specific code written for or running on the mobile devices that access it. What kind of mobile app might it be?

    A. mobile website;

    B. native;

    C. hybrid;

    D. no such mobile apps exist.

4 NECESSARY SKILLS

The learning objective for Chapter 1, Section 4, is recall of syllabus content only.

While we'll address the topic of skills in much more detail in Chapter 3, I bet you're starting to realize now that mobile testing is testing like any other testing, only more so. In other words, you'll need all the usual tester skills, plus some additional ones.

For example, the ISTQB® Foundation syllabus 2018 covers topics such as:

- requirements analysis;
- test design techniques;
- test environment and data creation;
- running tests;
- reporting results.

You'll need all of the skills covered in that syllabus. Also, since a lot of mobile software is developed following Lean, Agile, DevOps, or similar types of life cycles, there are Agile testing skills discussed in the ISTQB® Agile Tester Foundation syllabus 2014 that you should have.[4]

In addition to these device-independent skills, you need to think about the functional capabilities that are present in a mobile device but not in the standard PC or client–server or mainframe app.

For example, boundary value analysis is a useful test design technique, whether you're testing a mobile app or a mainframe app. However, if you're familiar with the old 3270 mainframe terminals, you can pick one of those up and twiddle it around at all sorts of different angles. It will still look the same and do the same things. Of course, in twiddling

---

[4] You can find a detailed explanation of the Agile Tester Foundation syllabus in Rex Black et al. (2017) *Agile Testing Foundations*. Swindon: BCS.

it around, you might well drop it on your foot and bust your toe, because a 3270 terminal weighs about 75 pounds. Fortunately, you don't have to put an accelerometer in something that's designed to sit on a desk and display EBCDIC characters in green letters.[5]

For those of you born a lot further away from the center of the last century than I was, consider the humble PC, desktop or laptop. Certainly, we're seeing some migration of mobile types of functionality into the PC, such as cellular network capability. However, most PCs still don't care whether you're touching their screens or tilting them one way or the other. Mobile devices do care, and they behave differently when you do.

These are significant functional differences that have testing implications. In addition, there are many, many quality characteristics above and beyond functionality, such as security, usability, performance, portability, compatibility, reliability, and so forth, that you must consider. You might be used to addressing these as part of testing PC apps or PC browser-based apps, but, if not, non-functional testing is something you'll need to study. I'll get you started on the important functional and non-functional mobile testing skills in Chapter 3, but there's lots to learn.

1.4 Test your knowledge

Let's try one or more sample exam questions related to the material we've just covered. The answers are found in Appendix C.

Question 6 Learning objective: recall of syllabus content only (K1)

A mobile tester can apply test techniques described in the Foundation and Test Analysis syllabi.

   A.   This statement is true, and no other techniques are required beyond those.
   B.   This statement is false, as mobile testing requires completely different techniques.
   C.   Since there are no best practices in mobile testing, only exploratory testing is used.
   D.   This statement is true, but additional techniques are needed for mobile testing.

5 EQUIPMENT REQUIREMENTS FOR MOBILE TESTING

The learning objective for Chapter 1, Section 5, is as follows:

MOB-1.5.1   (K2) Explain how equivalence partitioning can be used to select devices for testing.

---

[5] You might be thinking, "Wait, whoa, EBCDIC, 3270, mainframe? What is that stuff he's talking about?" Well, trust me, it was a thing, back in the day.

As you might have guessed from Section 3, equipment requirements pose major challenges for mobile application testing. As challenging as PC application compatibility testing can be, it's much more so with respect to mobile apps in many circumstances. While we cover this in more detail later, I'll introduce the challenge in this introductory chapter.

Whether you're creating a native mobile app, a hybrid app, or a mobile-optimized web app, the number of distinct configurations that your app could be run on is huge. Consider the factors: device firmware; operating system; operating system version; browser and browser version; potentially interoperating applications installed on the mobile device, such as a map application; and so on.

In these situations, you encounter what's called a combinatorial explosion. For example, suppose there are seven factors, and each factor has five possible options that you can choose. How many distinct configuration possibilities are there? Five to the seventh power, or 78,125 distinct configurations.

Obviously, complete coverage of all possible configurations is impractical. In Chapter 4, we'll examine in depth how to deal with these device configuration issues. However, for the moment, consider equivalence partitioning.

Instead of saying, "Yep, I'm gonna test all 78,000 possible configurations," you can say instead, "For each of these seven different factors, I'm gonna include in my test environment one device that has each of the five configuration options for each of the seven factors."

By doing so, you could get by with as few as five devices, depending on the factors. The risk is that, if any sort of combinatorial interactions happen, you won't catch those. For example, your app might work fine with all supported operating systems and with all supported mapping apps, but not with one particular operating system version together with a particular mapping version. Equivalence partitioning can't help you find this kind of bug, unless, through luck, that exact combination happens to be present in your test lab.

Now, there are techniques that can help you find pairwise bugs like this. In the ISTQB® Advanced Test Analyst syllabus 2018,[6] there's some discussion about pairwise techniques, which build upon equivalence partitioning. These techniques allow you to find certain combinatorial problems without committing to testing thousands of combinations.

In any case, when doing equivalence partitioning, it's important that you carefully consider all the relevant options for each factor. For example, is just one Android device sufficient to represent that operating system? Not always, for reasons we'll discuss in later chapters.

It's also important to consider factors above and beyond operating systems, browsers, interoperating applications and other software. For example, is the device at rest, is it moving at walking speed, is it moving at highway speed, or even is it moving at bullet train speed, if you're supporting Europe and Japan? Lighting can affect screen brightness and your ability to read the screen. Lighting tends to be different inside versus outside. If you're outside, is it day or night, sunny or overcast?

---

[6] See https://certifications.bcs.org/category/18218

So, what are the factors to consider? Here are some of them:

- the device manufacturer;
- the operating system and versions;
- the supported peripherals;
- whether the app is running on a phone or a tablet;
- which browser's being used;
- whether it's accessing the front or back camera, which might have different resolutions.

There are six factors here, but possibly hundreds of combinations. Rather than trying to test all possible combinations, you should ensure that you have one of each option for each factor present in the test environment.

1.5 Test your knowledge

Let's try one or more sample exam questions related to the material we've just covered. The answers are found in Appendix C.

Question 7 Learning objective: MOB-1.5.1 (K2) Explain how equivalence partitioning can be used to select devices for testing

How is equivalence partitioning useful in mobile testing?

    A. Mobile testers can only apply it to the selection of representative devices for testing, reducing test environment costs.

    B. Mobile testers can apply it to identify extreme values for configuration options, application settings, and hardware capacity.

    C. Mobile testers don't use equivalence partitioning in their testing work, but rather rely on mobile-specific techniques.

    D. Mobile testers can apply it to reduce the number of tests by recognizing situations where the application behaves the same.

6 LIFE CYCLE MODELS

The learning objective for Chapter 1, Section 6, is as follows:

MOB-1.6.1   (K2) Describe how some software development life cycle models are more appropriate for mobile applications.

Let's start at the beginning. Since the beginning of medium- to large-scale software development in the 1950s, development teams followed a development model similar to that used in civil engineering, electrical engineering, and mechanical engineering.

This model is sequential, starting with requirements identification, then design, then unit development and testing, then unit integration and testing, then system testing, and then, if relevant, acceptance testing. Each phase completes before the next phase starts.

In 1970, Winston Royce gave a presentation where he portrayed this sequential life cycle in a waterfall graphic. The name and the image, **waterfall**, stuck, and his name got stuck to the model. Because of this, poor Royce took the blame for years for the weaknesses of the waterfall model. Ironically, while the picture stuck, what Royce said didn't, because what he said was, "Don't actually do it like this, because you need iteration between the phases." When I studied software engineering in the 1980s at UCLA, my professor was careful to explain the iteration and overlap in the waterfall.

We also discussed Barry Boehm's spiral model, which uses a series of prototypes to iden-tify and resolve key technical challenges early in development.[7] In the early 1990s, in an attempt to put more structure around the iteration and overlap of the waterfall model and to incorporate Boehm's ideas about prototyping and stepwise refinement, practitioners like Philippe Kruchten, James Martin, and Steve McConnell advanced the traditional iterative models, Rational Unified Process and Rapid Application Development.[8] In these models, you break the set of features that you want to create into groups. Each group of features is built and tested in an iterative fashion. In addition, there is overlap between the different iterations; while developers are building one iteration, you're testing the previous iteration.

In the late 1990s, from the traditional iterative models emerged the various Agile tech-niques, and then in the 2000s Lean arrived, usually in the form of Kanban. These have in common the idea of breaking development work into very small iterations or even single features, building and testing those iterations or features, then delivering them.

Agile, Kanban, and Spiral are all capable of supporting rapid release of software. You release something, then build on that, then build on **that**, and so forth, over and over again. Done right, these models allow you to attain some degree of speed to market without totally compromising testing. However, a lot of app developers teeter on the jagged edge of this balance. Sometimes, in the rush to get something out, they short-circuit the testing.

It's really important as a tester, regardless of life cycle but especially when using life cycles that emphasize speed, such as Agile, Lean, and Spiral, to help people understand the risks they are taking. In addition, you can and should use techniques like risk-based testing to make sure that the most critical areas are tested sufficiently, and the less critical areas at least get some amount of attention.

The type of app matters. There might be less risk associated with a mass-market entertainment application like a video streaming app and more risk associated with a medical facility management app, such as the one I mentioned earlier in this chapter. With safety-critical software, regulations such as the Food and Drug Administration (FDA) regulations for medical systems come into play, which means a certain amount of documentation must be gathered to prove what you've tested. These types of factors

---

[7] Barry W. Boehm "A Spiral Model of Software Development and Enhancement". Available here: http://csse.usc.edu/ TECHRPTS/1988/usccse88-500/usccse88-500.pdf

[8] Steve McConnell's 1996 book *Rapid Development* (Redmond, WA: Microsoft Press) is a reference for RAD. Philippe Kruchten's 2003 book *The Rational Unified Process: An Introduction* (Boston, MA: Addison-Wesley Professional) is a reference for RUP.

might lead your organization to use a traditional iterative life cycle or even the classic waterfall.

> One bad habit that has become common in software engineering is what I'd call the spaghetti development model. This is based on the old line that the best way to check if spaghetti is done is to throw it against the wall to see if it sticks. In mobile development, people rationalize this by saying, "Hey, if we have a bad release, we can just do an Over The Air (OTA) update, pushing a fix to the people using the app."

Frankly, this is using customers as testers. Yes, it is possible to push fixes out fast in some cases. However, there's a famous quote from Ray Donovan, a businessman-turned-cabinet secretary accused of a massive fraud from his business days. After he was acquitted, he asked, "Where do I go to get my reputation back?"[9] Something to keep in mind. In the long run, I think such organizations will get a reputation for wasting their users' time and using them as a free test resource. Think: one-star reviews in the app store.

People have various degrees of tolerance for vendors wasting their time. I will admit to being completely intolerant of it. However, I think it's a mistake to assume that most people are at the other end of the spectrum, and will tolerate your organization doing regular OTA hose-downs with garbage software without posting a nasty review.

Consider Yelp, the social app for restaurant listings and other similar public venues. I like Yelp. I use it a fair amount. It isn't perfect and it sometimes has weird glitches related to location. However, for the most part it does what I need it to do.

I travel a lot, and I have to find a place to eat dinner. I'm not picky; I'm very open to eating many different kinds of food. However, I'm not open to the possibility of getting food-borne illness. That's not only inconvenient when traveling, it's exceptionally unpleasant and has a real impact on my ability to do my job and get paid. By using Yelp and its reviews, I can find food I'll enjoy that probably won't make me sick. Now, while I hate food poisoning, Yelp is not really a high-risk app. The quality is definitely in the good-enough category, not the bet-your-life category.

Contrast that with one of my clients that maintains a patient logging application. Doctors and patients use this app when they are testing a drug for safety and effectiveness. During the development of the drug, trial patients log their results and side effects. This information is used by the FDA to decide whether the drug can be released to the public. As such, this app is FDA regulated.

Obviously, it should get—and, I'm sure, does get—a much higher scrutiny than Yelp. That doesn't mean you can't use Agile methodologies. In fact, my client did use Agile for some period of time. They eventually went back to waterfall because it fit their release schedule better. However, either approach worked, as long as they gathered the necessary regulatory documentation.

---

[9] You can read *The New York Times* account of the outcome of Donovan's trial, and his comment about what the trial had done to his reputation, here: www.nytimes.com/1987/05/26/nyregion/donovan-cleared-of-fraud-charges-by-jury-in-bronx. html?pagewanted=all

1.6 Test your knowledge

Let's try one or more sample exam questions related to the material we've just covered. The answers are found in Appendix C.

Question 8 Learning objective: MOB-1.6.1 (K2) Describe how some software development life cycle models are more appropriate for mobile applications

Which of the following statements is true?

A. Agile life cycles are used for mobile app development because of the reduced need for regression testing associated with Agile life cycles.
B. Sequential life cycles are used for mobile app development because of the need for complete documentation of the tests.
C. Spiral models, with their rapid prototyping cycles, create too many technical risks for such life cycles to be used for mobile testing.
D. Mobile apps are often developed in a stepwise fashion, with each release adding a few new features as those features are built and tested.

In this chapter, we've introduced many of the topics we'll explore in this book. You saw the different types of mobile devices and mobile apps. Next, you saw what mobile users expect from their devices and the apps running on them. These mobile device and app realities, along with the expectations of the users, create challenges for testers, which you have overviewed here. You also briefly saw how mobile testing realities influence the topics of tester skills and equipment requirements. We closed by looking how the ongoing changes in the way software is built are influencing model app development. In the following chapters, we'll explore many of these topics in more detail, and look more closely at how mobile app testing differs from testing other kinds of software.

2 TEST PLANNING AND DESIGN

In this chapter, we address how to determine what to test, and how to test those things. We look at the how to identify the functions and attributes your app has, and what could go wrong with the app from a quality perspective. We then address how to determine when you've tested enough, which is always a difficult balancing act. We'll talk about how your test approach can be used to focus on that balance, covering the important test conditions. Finally, we'll address regression testing, an important topic with rapidly evolving mobile apps.

CHAPTER SECTIONS

Chapter 2, Test Planning and Design, contains the following six sections:

1. Identify functions and attributes
2. Identify and assess risks
3. Determine coverage goals
4. Determine test approach
5. Identify test conditions and set scope
6. Regression testing

CHAPTER TERMS

The terms to remember for Chapter 2 are as follows:

- minimal essential test strategy
- operational profiles
- risk analysis

1 IDENTIFY FUNCTIONS AND ATTRIBUTES

The learning objective for Chapter 2, Section 1, is as follows:

MOB-2.1.1   (K2) Explain why use cases are a good source of testing requirements for mobile applications.

As a comment on this learning objective, let me clarify the difference between use cases and user stories. They are not the same thing, even though some people use those phrases interchangeably. Let's review the ISTQB® definitions for each:

User story: A high-level user or business requirement commonly used in Agile software development, typically consisting of one or more sentences in the everyday or business language capturing what functionality a user needs, any non-functional criteria, and also includes acceptance criteria.

Use case: A sequence of transactions in a dialogue between an actor and a component or system with a tangible result, where an actor can be a user or anything that can exchange information with the system.

Now, it's not obvious from those definitions, but a use case is generally larger and more detailed than a user story. A use case is how an individual, often referred to as an actor, goes through a sequence of steps with the system to accomplish some task or achieve some goal. Those steps include steps in the normal workflow as well as steps that are part of exception workflows. Exception workflows include error handling resulting from disallowed inputs or actions, but also atypical but allowed inputs or actions. The focus of the use case is not only on the goal or task, but also on the process that plays out between system and actor.

A user story typically corresponds to a few steps from a use case, either steps that are part of the normal workflow or one of the exception workflows. A use case is much closer to what is sometimes called, in Agile terminology, an epic, which is a collection of related user stories. In addition, the focus is almost entirely on the goal or task to be accomplished, not on the steps taken to get there, which is why use cases are more detailed than a single user story or an epic.

Mobile devices tend to have a lot of features, and these features are available to mobile apps to use. This leads to some fundamental differences in both structure and behavior between mobile apps and standard PC apps. If you pick up your PC and stand it on its edge for example, it typically doesn't care that you're doing that, nor does it even have any way of knowing that you're doing that. So, the PC can't communicate that action to applications running on it.

However, the very power of many mobile apps derives from the fact that they can use all these different interesting sensors in the mobile devices they run on. Although, that's not true of all mobile apps. For example, Facebook and Twitter work much the same on a PC browser as they do on a mobile device, though the mobile apps' integration with geolocation and the camera makes some actions much more convenient. For a number of mobile apps, especially games, exploitation of many of the sensors and other mobile device features is key to the way the app works.

Now, you probably are less concerned about mobile device feature use in general than in the specific features used by your app. As part of planning and designing your tests, you need to think about the mobile-specific features your app uses, including the sensors. You need to think about how those features and sensors affect your app and the way it behaves, in the context of the different important quality characteristics your app has. We'll address quality characteristics and how to focus on the important ones later.

In traditional life cycles, you could sometimes rely on getting a fully defined, detailed set of requirements specifications to help you understand the app's intended behaviour. If you're testing a regulated device or app, as discussed earlier, that might well happen.[1] However, most mobile app development proceeds in a much more lightweight, low-documentation fashion, often following or adapting Agile methods. So, expect to get either use cases or user stories, depending on the team you're working with and their chosen life cycle.

Remember, as a tester, you have to play the hand you're dealt. If all you get are emails from developers with subject lines like, "Descriptions of all the cool stuff I built last night," then roll with it.

Regardless of whether you receive unstructured emails, use cases, user stories, or traditional specifications, often the focus is on the functionality. Non-functional behaviors, such as performance, reliability, usability, and portability, might be under-specified or entirely unspecified. You must recognize when there's missing information and discover ways to pull that information from whatever sources are available for it.

Not only must you remember to get details on non-functional behavior, you also must have the ability to test non-functional behavior. Performance, reliability, and usability can be particularly challenging, so I will return to those topics in more detail later.

Table 2.1 Informal use case for navigational app

Use case: Set destination

Normal workflow

1. User enters their desired destination
2. App confirms the destination from user
3. User refines destination information, submits to app
4. App retrieves current location and relevant map, displays possible routes
5. User confirms route app is to use

Exceptions

- App unable to retrieve location information; fail
- App unable to retrieve relevant map; fail
- User does not refine destination information; timeout and exit
- User does not confirm route; timeout and exit

[1] Though even in such environments, documentation is not perfect. As one reviewer of this book wrote, "Regulated apps [sometimes] fall short of receiving solid use cases, requirements, or even functional specs. [There can be a] lack of expected behavior and thus requirements are not fleshed out until software is developed and tested ... Testers may need to provide information about limitations, boundaries and baselines."

Table 2.1 shows an example of a use case for a navigational app. One important task in such an app is setting a desired destination, which is a necessary part of finding directions to that destination.

The normal workflow starts with the user entering a destination, such as a restaurant name. The app confirms the user's selection, which often involves having the user select from a list of matching addresses or simply confirming the address the app found. The app then checks the current location using device sensors, retrieves the relevant map, and finds possible routes. The app comes back to the user, who selects the chosen route. This is the normal workflow, sometimes called the happy path.

Various things can happen along that path, some of which aren't so happy. Perhaps the device can't get the current location information. Perhaps it can't find a relevant map. In either case, it will fail and return the appropriate error message. Perhaps the user doesn't respond in the dialog, which would result in a timeout and exit.

To go back to a point I made earlier in this section, suppose we wanted to break this use case down into user stories. One user story within this use case might read, "As a user, I want to submit partial destination information, so that I can select my final destination." This user story corresponds to steps one, two and three of this use case.

Returning to the topic at hand, testing, how can we use a use case like this one for testing? The usual coverage rule is to have at least one test for the normal workflow, and at least one test for each of the exceptions. It often makes sense to apply equivalence partitioning to the workflows, too. For example, we should test with a full address and at least one partial address. We should test with at least one business and at least one residence.

The process for translating use cases into test cases is described in more detail in the ISTQB®'s Advanced Test Analyst syllabus 2018, as well as my book and course that cover that syllabus.[2]

> As a note for the exam, throughout this book I'll use phrases like **use case, decision table, equivalence partitioning, boundary value analysis**, and **state transition diagrams**. If it's been a long time since you took the ISTQB® Certified Tester Foundation exam, or you never took the exam, you might be rusty on these terms and the test design techniques associated with them.
>
> If so, start by reading Chapter 4 in the ISTQB® Foundation syllabus 2018.[3] Next, check to be sure that, for all the techniques discussed in Chapter 4, you can apply those techniques. It's very likely that you will see some questions on the ASTQB Mobile Tester exam that involve applying the ISTQB® black-box test design techniques discussed in the ISTQB® Foundation syllabus 2018.

---

[2] My book on the Advanced Test Analyst syllabus is *Advanced Software Testing: Volume 1* (second edition, 2015 San Rafael, CA: Rocky Nook), and my company offers an Advanced Test Analyst course as well.
[3] See the ISTQB® Certified Tester Foundation syllabus 2018 here: https://certifications.bcs.org/upload/pdf/swt-foundation-syllabus.pdf

2.1 Test your knowledge

Let's try one or more sample exam questions related to the material we've just covered. The answers are found in Appendix C.

Question 1 Learning objective: MOB-2.1.1 (K2) Explain why use cases are a good source of testing requirements for mobile applications

Why do use cases help you test mobile applications?

- A. Use cases help developers build an application that meets the users' needs.
- B. Use cases should be used to identify how certain conditions result in certain actions.
- C. Use cases help you focus on what users want to accomplish with the application.
- D. Use cases should be used to create operational profiles for performance and reliability testing.

2 IDENTIFY AND ASSESS RISKS

The learning objective for Chapter 2, Section 2, is as follows:

MOB-2.2.1   (K2) Describe different approaches to risk analysis.

This learning objective relates to another technique described in the ISTQB® Certified Tester Foundation syllabus 2018, which is risk-based testing, covered in Chapter 5. You should read this section of the syllabus if you're not familiar with it, or it's been a long time since you went through it. In addition, if you want further information about risk-based testing, there are a number of articles, templates, videos, and recorded webinars on the RBCS website (www.rbcs-us.com) which you can access free.

Let's start by defining a risk. We can informally define risk as a possible negative outcome. The two key elements in this definition are possibility and negativity. A risk is neither impossible nor certain. If a risk becomes an outcome, that outcome is undesirable. Risks are of different levels, as we know from real life.

For any realistic-sized system, testing cannot reduce the risk of failure in production to zero, due to the impossibility of exhaustive testing. While testing does reduce the risk of failure in production, most approaches to testing reduce risk in a suboptimal and opaque fashion.

Risk-based testing allows you to select test conditions, allocate effort for each condition, and prioritize the conditions in such a way as to maximize the amount of risk reduction obtained for any given amount of testing. Further, risk-based testing allows reporting of test results in terms of which risks have been mitigated and which risks have not.

Risk-based testing starts with a process of analyzing risk to the quality of the system. First, you work with your fellow project team members to identify what could go wrong with the system. These are the quality risks, or, to use another common name, the product risks. For a map app that gives walking or driving directions, examples would include failure to properly determine location, failure to display distance in the default units (for example, metric versus imperial), and use of a too-small font that makes street names and landmark names difficult to read. In risk-based testing, these quality risks are potential test conditions. To determine which of the risks are test conditions, you and your colleagues assess the level of each risk. Important risks will be tested. The testing effort associated with each risk depends on its level of risk. The order in which a risk is tested depends on its level of risk, too.

The easiest way to assess the level of risk is to use two factors: likelihood and impact. Likelihood has to do with the odds of a risk becoming an outcome. Impact has to do with the financial, reputational, safety, mission, and business consequences if the risk does become an outcome.

For example, people buy life insurance for premature death. As the saying goes, insurance is a bet that you want to lose. For all insurance, it's likely that you will pay more than you ever collect, and you're happy if that's the case. Hopefully, premature death is unlikely, unless you engage in highly self-destructive lifestyle behaviors. (In that case, the life insurance companies won't insure you.) So, premature death has a low likelihood. However, the impact can be very high. For example, suppose you are a primary breadwinner for your family, you have three kids, all under 18, and you die. Unless you have life insurance—or you had the good sense to be born with inherited wealth—that will be a devastating event for your family.

It can work the other way, too. For example, in many places in the world, going outside in the summer involves the risk of sunburn. The likelihood is very high. Usually—barring unusual disease outbreaks—the impact is very low. So, this is a risk managed through clothing and sunscreen, rather than insurance.

Testing software prior to release reduces the likelihood of undetected, serious bugs escaping into production; that is, it reduces risk to overall system quality. Anything that could go wrong and reduce product quality, that's a quality risk.

When thinking of quality risks, think broadly. Consider all features and attributes that can affect customer, user, and stakeholder satisfaction. Consider the project team, the IT organization, and the entire company. Quality, to use J.M. Juran's definition, is fitness for use, which is the presence of attributes that satisfy stakeholders and the absence of attributes that would dissatisfy them.[4]

---

[4] Juran's definition of quality can be found in his 1992 book *Juran on Quality by Design: The New Steps for Planning Quality into Goods and Services* (Free Press: New York).

Another useful definition of quality, from Phil Crosby, is conformance to requirements, which is software that behaves the way use cases, user stories, design documents, public claims of capability (for example, on websites and sales materials), and other such documents describe.[5]

Bugs can cause the software to fail to meet requirements or to exhibit other dissatisfying behaviors. Bugs can affect functional or non-functional behaviors. When you're doing risk analysis, don't just think about functional quality risks. Think about non-functional quality risks as well.

In addition to quality risks, there is another kind of risk, called project risks. Project risks are bad things that could happen that would affect your ability to carry out the project successfully.

Here are some examples of quality risks:

- app soft keyboard input appears very slowly in field during login;
- app cannot find a location when using network (rather than GPS) for location information;
- app crashes if Wi-Fi or cellular data connectivity is lost during account creation.

Here are some examples of project risks:

- key project participant quits prior to the end of the project;
- equipment needed for testing not delivered in time;
- project sponsors cancel project funding during project.

Risk-based testing is primarily about mitigating quality risks through testing prior to release. However, proper management of testing requires management of test-related project risks too.

Examples of mobile app quality risks in different categories

Mobile apps can be affected by a variety of quality risks across various categories. To help spur your thinking, here are some examples, for a mobile ecommerce app:

- **Functional:** inaccurately calculates tax on purchases;
- **Localization:** does not use the proper currency;
- **Reliability:** app crashes on launch or during usage;
- **Performance:** app responds too slowly during checkout;

---

[5] You can find this definition of quality, along with a number of other useful ideas, in Phil Crosby's 1979 book *Quality Is Free* (New York: McGraw-Hill).

- **Usability:** customer confused by put-in-cart dialog boxes;
- **Portability:** app works incorrectly on Android devices;
- **Physical:** app cannot use location information to determine proper locale;
- **Error handling:** customer able to submit invalid purchase information.

As I mentioned, these are only examples. Your app's specific risks will vary, and may include risks in other categories as well as the ones listed above.

How to identify and assess quality risks

As I said before, you must consider functional and non-functional risks. You also need to consider physical aspects, the ways in which the mobile app interacts with the physical world via the device's sensors.

One of the mistakes testers sometimes make when they start doing risk-based testing is to sit down alone and say, "Right, I'll just take all the requirements, and then ask myself, for each requirement, what could go wrong. Voila! Those are the risks." While it is true that those are **some** of the risks, those are not **all** of the risks. Why? Because the requirements are imperfect and incomplete, and your personal understanding of the project and product is also imperfect and incomplete.

You can address this by including business and technical stakeholders in the risk identification and assessment process. This is harnessing the wisdom of the crowd to reach a better decision than any one person, no matter how smart, could. The inclusion of a wide range of stakeholders is another reason why you need to use a lightweight, quality risk analysis process. Busy stakeholders will not participate in a process seen as a high-overhead, low-value process encumbrance.

While we'll return to the topic of non-functional quality attributes in the next chapter, right now let's focus on the intersection of physical and functional attributes, and thus the quality risks present at those intersections.

On the functional side, there's what the software can do, its features, the problems it can solve, the entertainment it can provide, what the display looks like, and so forth. It might have audio elements to it, such as the ability to play music or take voice instructions. It might have visual elements, from simple visual cues to the ability to stream videos. There can be tactile elements, both in terms of you providing input via the touchscreen and the app providing output by vibrating.

These functional elements can be cross-referenced with the physical elements that interact with them. You can put together a matrix showing intersections between functional elements and the physical elements, for example, different buttons, icons, and graphics that produce and are produced by certain features, the way that the battery and power management change the way the functionality behaves, the way the app uses rotational sensors, accelerometers, location information, and cameras, and any other sort of physical sensor the device has. Notice that these physical elements are not functions on their own, but they are used by the functions, and many of the functions won't work without them. Therefore, using a matrix to identify these physical/functional interactions can help you see risks.

When you assess likelihood and impact of a risk, if you have an app that's already out in production, you should look at production metrics. While I can't give you an exhaustive list of metrics, here are some ideas:

- How many times has your app been downloaded? This applies to a native app. With a mobile website, you might look at the number of registered users.

- What is the number of downloads versus active application users? Obviously, if you have a relatively high number of downloads, but a low number of application users, that could indicate problems that are leading to a low active user rate.

- You can look at new users versus lost users, with the lost users being the difference between the total downloads and the active application users. You want the new user numbers to be high relative to the lost users, and the lost user numbers to be as low as possible.

- Frequency of use is another metric to consider. How often people do certain kinds of things is important to keep in mind. Obviously, the screens and features that are more frequently used have higher risk from an impact point of view. If they're broken, then that creates more problems for people.

- Consider depth of visit and duration. How much time do people spend on the app, and what do they do? What kind of screens do they visit? This depends on your app, too. For example, with Yelp, if Yelp is doing its job right, you should be able to get in and out of that app quickly. In a matter of a minute or maybe less, you should be able to find the restaurant that you want, or the nightclub that you want. So, it might indicate a problem if Yelp had a very high depth of visit numbers versus Facebook, for example. Facebook wants you to buy stuff from their advertisers, so, to expose you to lots of ads, they want you to stick around. They want long duration and deep depth of visit.

- If you have a high bounce rate—the "I tried it once, and I've never used it again" number—there's clearly something wrong with your app. What is wrong isn't necessarily obvious. Is it reliability, is it performance, is it usability, or is it absence of functionality? Clearly, something is wrong, because a high bounce rate means people hate your app.

So, these are some metrics to consider. There are also metrics discussed in the ISTQB® Certified Tester Foundation syllabus 2018, the ISTQB® Agile Tester syllabus 2014,[6] and the ISTQB® Certified Advanced Test Manager syllabus 2012[7] with respect to risk analysis that are worth taking a look at.

The process of risk-based testing

Let's summarize the risk-based software testing process. We analyze the quality risks, identifying the risks, and then assess their level based on likelihood and impact. Based

---

[6] See https://certifications.bcs.org/category/18255
[7] See https://certifications.bcs.org/category/18219

on the level of risk, we will determine what to test, how much, and in what order. By doing so, we will minimize the residual level of risk for the system as a whole.

In the case of mobile app testing, the process must involve very lightweight techniques, because of the time pressures involved and the iterative life cycles often used. In addition, the risk analysis process should feed into the estimation process, since risk analysis determines the overall effort needed for testing. Likewise, the estimation techniques also need to be lightweight, again due to time and life cycle constraints.

Interconnecting risk analysis and estimation provides a clean way for the project team to collectively determine what to test, how much, and in what order. With that done, you can design and create a set of tests that cover the identified risks. The coverage for each risk is based on the level of risk. You then run those tests in a sequence based on the level of risk, too.

The life cycle influences the way risk-based testing works. In a sequential life cycle, quality risk analysis occurs at the beginning of the project and everything follows from that for the next three months, six months, or even a year. However, for most mobile app development, you won't have a one-year-long development effort. For example, if you are using Agile or some similar process, quality risk analysis happens at the beginning of each iteration, as part of the iteration planning process.

Based on your risk analysis, the higher the risk, the more you test and the earlier you test. The lower the risk, the less you test and the later you test. The sequencing of the tests is clear, as you simply group the tests by the level of risk associated with the risks they cover, then run them in order of the level of risk. (I'm simplifying a bit here, since the arrival of new features in an iteration creates regression risk for features already tested, and some attention must be paid to the regression risks. We'll return to this topic later.)

Next, we have to consider, on a certain level of risk, what that means in terms of the number of tests to create. Unfortunately, the mapping of level-of-risk to level-of-test-effort isn't a simple calculation. Fortunately, I have an article on my website about selection of test design techniques based on the level of risk. It's called "Matching Test Techniques to the Extent of Testing." It's only four pages long, and will give you some insights for effort allocation.[8]

Now, I said that prioritization of testing based on risk is clear, and that's true. It's very easy to determine the theoretical order in which you'll run the tests. However, you can't test software until you receive it, so risk-based test prioritization often requires risk-based development prioritization. This is true because most of the time you'll work in an iterative or incremental type of life cycle. Features are delivered to you for testing as they are completed. If features are built out of risk order, you can't run your tests in risk order.

You may be familiar with the phrase **forcing function** with respect to usability. It refers to the way an app guides someone toward the right way to use it. You've encountered

---

[8] You can find the article mentioned here: https://rbcs-us.com/resources/articles/matching-test-techniques-to-the-extent-of-testing/

the forcing function if you ever think, as you're using an app, "Yes, it's just so obvious. In order to access that feature, you do this, then you do this, then you do this." You might not even notice when the app is easy to use, just like a fish probably doesn't notice the water as long as it's in it.

However, like a fish out of water, you're quite likely to notice the absence of the forcing function, because the absence will be experienced as frustration. You know those feelings, I'm sure. The "what is it doing?" and "what am I supposed to do next here?" feelings.

You can think of risk as a forcing function. Risk should guide you in your decisions about what to test, in what order, and how much. If you are doing safety critical or mission critical applications, you might use a formal risk analysis technique such as Failure Mode and Effect Analysis, which involves identifying not only risks, but the potential causes of those risks and how those risks would affect stakeholders. However, it's more likely you'll use a lightweight technique, such as Pragmatic Risk Analysis and Management (PRAM), a technique I've been using for 20-plus years, which is what is described here. Such lightweight techniques don't create a lot of documentation. You can capture their outputs on a spreadsheet or even a paper-based task-board.[9]

Structuring the quality risk analysis

Figure 2.1 shows a template that you can use to capture your risk analysis information, if you use the PRAM technique. You can find a list of general-quality risk categories in Table 2.2. You should use that list as the starting point for your risk identification process, working through it with your stakeholders. As you work through the checklist, you will populate the left column of the template. Remember that not all quality risk categories will apply to your app. Review them, select the categories that do, and then, in each risk category, identify the specific risks.

Once you have identified the risks, you can populate the likelihood and the impact columns as you assess the level of risk for each risk item. I use a five-point scale for likelihood and impact. The scales run from very high to very low for both likelihood and impact.

For likelihood, usually, interpreting the scale is relatively straightforward. How likely is it that we would have bugs related to this risk item in our product? How often have we seen similar bugs in the past?[10]

In terms of impact, though, distinguishing very high impact, from high impact, from medium impact, from low impact, from very low impact, that varies quite a bit from company to company, and app to app. So, when you first start using risk-based testing, work with your stakeholders to create well-defined criteria for those different impact levels to make sure that everybody is speaking the same language.

---

[9] You can find a good description of Pragmatic Risk Analysis and Management (PRAM) in my 2014 book *Advanced Software Testing: Volume 2* (second edition, San Rafael, CA: Rocky Nook). Failure Mode and Effect Analysis is described in D.H. Stamatis's 2003 book *Failure Mode and Effect Analysis: FMEA from Theory to Execution* (Milwaukee, WI: American Society for Quality Press).

[10] It is important to note that likelihood does not refer to the frequency of the failure's occurrence in actual use. Frequency of occurrence is a consideration when evaluating impact, since this is a question of defect importance.

Figure 2.1 A quality risk analysis template

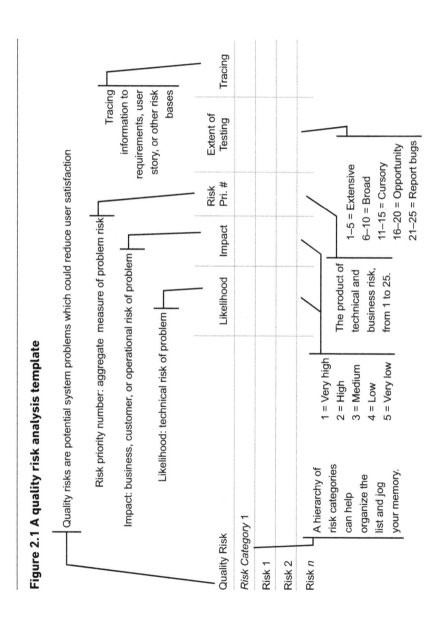

Table 2.2 Quality risk categories

Quality risk category	What kind of problems fit into this category
Competitive inferiority	Failures to match competing systems in quality.
Data quality	Failures in processing, storing, or retrieving data.
Date and time handling	Failures in date-based and/or time-based inputs/outputs, calculations, and event handling.
Disaster handling and recovery	Failure to degrade gracefully in the face of catastrophic incidents and/or failure to recover properly from such incidents.
Documentation	Failures in operating instructions for users or system administrators.
Error handling and recovery	Failures due to foreseeable mistakes such as user input errors.
Functionality	Failures that cause specific features not to work, either in terms of giving the wrong answer or not solving the problem.
Installation, setup, upgrade, and migration	Failures that prevent or impede deploying the system, migrating data to new versions, including unwanted side effects (for example, installing of additional, unwelcome, unintended software such as spyware, malware, etc.).
Interoperability	Failures that occur when major components, subsystems, or related systems interact.
Load, capacity, and volume	Failures in scaling of system to expected peak concurrent usage levels.
Localization	Failures in specific localities, including languages, messages, taxes and finances, operational issues, and time zones.
Networked and distributed	Failure to handle networked/distributed operation, including latency, delays, lost packet/connectivity, and unavailable resources.
Operations and maintenance	Failures that endanger continuing operation, including backup/restore processes.
Packaging/fulfillment	Failures associated with the packaging and/or delivery of the system or product.
Performance	Failures to perform (i.e. response time, throughput, and/or resource utilization) as required under expected loads.
Portability, configuration, and compatibility	Failures specific to different supported platforms, supported configurations, configuration problems, and/or cohabitation with other software/systems.

(Continued)

Table 2.2 (Continued)

Quality risk category	What kind of problems fit into this category
Reliability, availability, and stability	Failures to meet reasonable expectations of availability, mean time between failure, and recovery from foreseeable adverse events.
Security/privacy	Failures to protect the system and secured data from fraudulent or malicious misuse, problems with availability, violations of relevant security or privacy regulations, and similar issues.
Standards compliance	Failure to conform to mandatory standards, company standards, and/or applicable voluntary standards.
States and transactions	Failure to properly respond to sequences of events or to particular transactions.
User interface and usability	Failures in human factors, especially at the user interface.

By the way, notice I use a descending scale, so as the numbers go up, the level of risk goes down. If you don't like that, you can flip these around and have five be very high, and one be very low. Either way, you have numbers ranging from one to five in the Likelihood column and in the Impact column.

So, now you've assessed likelihood and impact, each rated on a five-point scale from one to five. Using a formula in this spreadsheet, in the Risk Priority Number column, you can simply multiply likelihood and impact. That calculation gives you an aggregate measure of risk. I call that the risk priority number.

So, assuming a descending scale, consider a risk with a risk priority of number one. Here's a risk that is very likely to happen. In addition, it's a risk with a very high impact. In other words, this risk is associated with a failure that could potentially pose an existential crisis to the company if it occurs in production.

Compare that to a risk with a risk priority number of 25. It's very unlikely to happen and has a very low impact. In other words, very few people would be affected by it, and even those people wouldn't care much.

At this point, it becomes clear how risk can guide our testing. Something with a risk priority number of 1, super scary and almost certain to happen, well, we better test the hell out of that, because, if we miss serious bugs in that area, we're in big trouble later. Something with a risk priority number of 25, utterly trivial and almost certain not to happen, well, maybe we get around to testing that, maybe not.

There are also a couple of other extremes possible, related to risks that are very likely but with very low potential impact and risks that are very unlikely but with very high potential impact. You'll need to consider carefully how to deal with such situations, especially with safety-critical or mission-critical systems where very high impact can mean death or the loss of millions of dollars.

Given the risk priority number, we can use that number to sequence tests. Tests that cover a risk with a risk priority number closer to 1 get run earlier. Tests that cover a risk with a risk priority number closer to 25 get run later—if at all. Remember, the risk priority number is heuristic, and the level of risk can change, so be flexible in the use of this rule of thumb.

So that's test prioritization, but how about allocation of test effort? As you can see, I've given the extent of testing based on ranges of risk priority number. There are five levels of test effort allocation: extensive, broad, cursory, opportunity, and report bugs only. (These correspond to the levels of effort described in the article I mentioned earlier, "Matching Test Techniques to the Extent of Testing", available on the RBCS website.)

The particular size of the ranges associated with each level of test effort allocation can vary, so consider what's shown here only an example. In this example, if the risk priority number for a particular risk is anywhere from 1 to 5, there will be extensive testing on that risk. If the risk priority number is 6 to 10, there will be broad testing. If the risk priority number is 11 to 15, there will be cursory testing. If the risk priority number is 16 to 20, you look for opportunities to test that risk as part of something else, but it doesn't get its own tests. And if the risk priority number is 21 to 25, there will be little to no testing, but you will report bugs related to this risk if you see them.

Finally, at the rightmost side of the template is the Tracing column. If your risks are based on user stories, use cases, requirements, and so forth, then you capture that traceability information here. Now, you might say, "Wait a minute, I think you just contradicted yourself, Rex, because you said earlier that you just look at requirements when you're analyzing risks. You talk to stakeholders, too."

Yes, that is true. You start off by talking to people. You interview business and technical stakeholders to identify the risks, and assess their level of risk. Once you've done that, you go through the use cases, the user stories, what have you, and establish the relationship between the requirements that you have—in whatever form—and the risks that you've identified. If you come across a requirement that doesn't relate to any identified risk, you should add risks for that requirement because you're missing risks.

It's also possible that you will have risks that don't relate to a specific requirement. You might say that's a problem with the requirements. And you might be right about that. And maybe that's a problem that needs to be fixed. But it's outside the scope of testing. So, I'd suggest that, if you find risks that don't relate to any specific requirement, you report those risks to the people who own the requirements—say, the product owner in a Scrum life cycle—and let them solve the problem.

2.2 Test your knowledge

Let's try one or more sample exam questions related to the material we've just covered. The answers are found in Appendix C.

Question 2 Learning objective: MOB-2.2.1 (K2) Describe different approaches to risk analysis

Assume that you have been asked to determine the testing needed for a brand-new mobile application. It will run on Apple and Android phones and tablets, and will allow users to purchase movie tickets online, including reserving seats and ordering food in advance. Because complex graphics are used during seat selection, speed of connection is important. Because transactions must be atomic—that is, either seats are reserved and paid for or no seat is reserved and no charge is made—reliability and performance matter.

What would be a good first step towards a risk analysis for this application?

A. Consider production metrics related to usability and performance.
B. Schedule a risk-identification brainstorming session with other project participants.
C. Assess the likelihood and impact of each risk using a four-point scale from critical to low.
D. Identify examples of risks based on physical, functional, and non-functional aspects.

3 DETERMINE COVERAGE GOALS

The learning objective for Chapter 2, Section 3, is as follows:

MOB-2.3.1 (K2) Explain how coverage goals will influence the level and type of testing to be conducted.

So, you've done your risk analysis, and you know the risks and their associated level of risk. Now you need to think of what I refer to as dimensions of coverage. These are the different things you need to cover in your tests and how deeply you will need to cover them.

Once again, project and product stakeholders need to be part of this process, determining what to test. Collectively, we must determine coverage goals so that we can all say, "Yes, this is what we need to test and this is how much we need to test it." It must be a collective decision, because there's usually a balance to be struck between, on the one hand, "are we covering enough to reduce the level of risk to an acceptable level?", versus, on the other hand, "can we actually get all this testing done?"

Reaching that decision is likely somewhat iterative. What you first suggest from a coverage point of view and what you ultimately arrive at are not the same thing. As test professionals, we tend to want more testing, while product people, marketing people and sales people, well, they often want to have their cake and eat it too, which means pressure to finish quicker.

Determining the relevant dimensions of mobile test coverage

What do I mean by **dimensions of coverage**? Well, the obvious dimensions of coverage are things like requirements, user stories, and use cases. This is often where people stop. They say, "I tested the requirements, I tested the use cases, I tested the user stories. What else is there?" Well, remember, requirements are always incomplete and imperfect. So, certainly, you must do verification of whatever requirements you've received. And, when you do that, you need traceability between your tests and the requirements they cover, so that, when the requirements change, you can make some educated guesses about what to do from a regression testing point of view, as well as figuring out what tests to update.

The quality risks that you identified in Section 2 are another dimension of testing. As I mentioned in that section, you should have traceability between your tests and your risks. So again, you might need to make some updates to your tests, and you might need to do some more regression testing based on that.

Major functional areas are another important dimension. It's possible that this dimension is already handled by the requirements and risks, but you should check for complete coverage.

Now, I would hope that your developers are using automated unit testing, included in some sort of continuous integration framework. If so, they should be looking at code coverage. In my opinion, they should achieve 100 percent branch coverage, also called decision coverage, in their code. If they're not, there are important paths in the code that are not being tested, and that's an incompletely covered dimension of testing.

You should also look at bug taxonomies. There are various bug taxonomies that you can find on the internet to give you some ideas. Bug taxonomies are basically classifications of bugs that you have seen in the past. There's always a chance one of those bugs could come back and bite you again.[11]

Similarly, consider technical debt. These are areas of the product that you know have weaknesses. Test those weaknesses.

Consider the different supported devices for the product. We'll come back to this again later, but at the very least you want to cover the equivalence partitions discussed in the

---

[11] The original bug taxonomy was included by Boris Beizer in 1990, in one of the fundamental and still relevant books on testing, *Software Testing Techniques* (New York: Van Nostrand Reinhold). I reproduced this in my own 2009 book *Managing the Testing Process, Third Edition* (Hoboken, NJ: John Wiley & Sons). Cem Kaner and Giri Vijayaraghavan published a detailed paper on the generation of such taxonomies in 2003 which you can find here: www.testingeducation.org/articles/bug_taxonomies_use_them_to_generate_better_tests_star_east_2003_paper.pdf

previous chapter, and possibly even pairwise testing if you're worried about combinational issues.

Since we're talking about mobile apps, you must consider different forms of connectivity. Again, we'll come back to this later, but think about how your app communicates. It's probably not just through Wi-Fi. There might be cellular; there might be Bluetooth; there might be other forms of communication.

Geography can be another dimension. If your app will be used internationally, there are different types of connectivity in different countries, and your GPS information will be different.

Your users are also a dimension of coverage. Have you identified all your different groups of users? Have you identified their capabilities? Do you know what they're likely to know, and not to know? What are the personas that they have? Are they patient? Are they impatient? How do they interact with software? What operational profiles—that is, the mixes of transactions and users that will be active at any given moment—are likely to affect your servers?

These are just some dimensions. Not all of these will necessarily apply, and there might be others that will apply that aren't listed here, so you need to consider them. The more dimensions that are applicable, the more breadth of testing is required. The higher the risk in any of these areas, the more in depth you need to go. As the depth and the breadth of testing expand, the testing effort increases, the number of necessary test environments increases, and the duration increases. So, we're back to negotiating a balance with your stakeholders.

For example, consider how coverage goals can vary across two apps. Suppose I've got an app developed for use in businesses engaged in senior care, assisted living, and so forth. The app will be used by the senior person. It manages their medical stats; for example, having the user take their blood pressure readings and enter them daily. It reminds them of medications and doctor's appointments. It tracks their exercise and what they ate. All this personal information gets stored on a central server for various kinds of data analytics.

Contrast that against an informational app that has no storage of any sort of data related to people on a central server. The informational app allows you to subscribe to various kinds of newsfeeds from different news providing web services.

Obviously, your relevant test dimensions for these two apps are very different. What are the different types of testing that need to be performed and how much? For example, is security an issue for the informational app? Not really. However, security is a huge issue for the personal health app. For one thing, there's a regulatory consideration for that app with respect to the Health Insurance Portability and Accountability Act in the United States and similar rules about personal medical information in the UK.

Similarly, usability considerations are very different. Seniors might have various kinds of limitations on what they can do with their hands. You can't use small buttons and checkboxes and so forth, and, while the features could be complicated, the user interface can't be.

The risks are quite different. There's a fairly simple set of risks for the informational app. There's a more complex set of risks for the personal health app, and the risks are a lot higher. Suppose the health app loses track of somebody's medications and stops reminding that person to take their blood pressure medication. Bam! They have a stroke.

For each app, we need to consider who's using it, and when are they using it. The whole operational profile mix is different. The profile will be very cyclical with the health app versus event driven for the informational app.

So, the testing necessary is very, very different for these two apps. It's definitely not one size fits all.

2.3 Test your knowledge

Let's try one or more sample exam questions related to the material we've just covered. The answers are found in Appendix C.

Question 3 Learning objective: MOB-2.3.1 (K2) Explain how coverage goals will influence the level and type of testing to be conducted

Assume that you have been asked to determine the testing needed for a brand-new mobile application. It will run on Apple and Android phones and tablets, and will allow users to purchase movie tickets online, including reserving seats and ordering food in advance. Because complex graphics are used during seat selection, speed of connection is important. Because transactions must be atomic—that is, either seats are reserved and paid for or no seat is reserved and no charge is made—reliability and performance matter.

Information related to which of the following coverage goals is mentioned in this scenario?

    A. connectivity;
    B. risks;
    C. code;
    D. no coverage-related information is mentioned.

Question 4 Learning objective: term understanding (K1)

What is an operational profile?

    A. The representation of a distinct set of tasks performed by the component or system, possibly based on user behavior when interacting with the component or system, and their probabilities of occurrence.
    B. Hardware and software products installed at users' or customers' sites where the component or system under test will be used. The software may include operating systems, database management systems, and other applications.

C. Testing conducted to evaluate a component or system in its operational environment.

D. A black-box test design technique where test cases are selected, possibly using a pseudo-random generation algorithm, to test non-functional attributes such as reliability and performance.

4 DETERMINE TEST APPROACH

The learning objective for Chapter 2, Section 4, is recall of syllabus content only.

So far in this chapter, we have discussed determining what the app does, using that information to identify and assess the risks that exist for the app, and in turn using that information, together with other sources of information, to identify what we wish to cover – our coverage goals. As the saying goes, though, if wishes were fishes none of us would starve.

To put our coverage goals into action, you need a strategy, and further you need a specific way to implement your strategy for the current project. The ISTQB® term for the implementation of a test strategy is *test approach*, so that's the term I'll use here. If you are unclear about test strategies, test approaches and test plans, you should pause reading this book and review Chapter 5 of the ISTQB® Foundation syllabus before continuing with this section.

Assuming you are up to speed on test approaches, let's discuss what you need to cover in a mobile app test approach. Environments are a main consideration, of course. You need to determine the different devices needed for testing and where you will get them. We'll return to this topic in detail later in this book, when we discuss the factors that influence choices of purchased devices, rented devices, cloud devices, simulators, and emulators. Environments includes peripherals, too, if your app supports them; items such as Bluetooth keyboards, flat-screen televisions (for HDMI connections or IR control), and so forth.

You need to take into account your users and other people issues. For your users, consider their personas, abilities, and disabilities. For example, remember the hypothetical senior health app I discussed earlier. Older people tend to have eyesight limitations and mobility limitations, and may have much less exposure to technology. How will your testing take that into account?

Another approach consideration is what's sometimes called the application domain or alternatively the industry context. This includes the business problem solved by the app and what considerations exist there. For example, if you are testing a banking app, security is huge. So, you have to consider how you will test things like authentication, susceptibility to man-in-the-middle attacks, and many other security concerns. It might be that you don't have the expertise to do security testing, so you might need to engage a security testing expert.

You should also consider the issue of what is in scope and out of scope as part of your approach. For example, in some organizations, different teams handle security and usability. In that case, these two areas of testing should be explicitly out of scope in your test approach.

As I've mentioned before, it's likely that we'll need to achieve a balance between what we'd like to test and what we actually can test, given the constraints of schedule and budget. Your test approach should address that.

The test approach should identify the test oracles. A test oracle is something that you can consult to determine the expected result of a test. Certainly, the oracles include the requirements, but, as I said earlier, most requirements are incomplete and imperfect. So, other oracles include previous releases of your app, competitors' apps, industry standards, and common user expectations related to performance, reliability, and usability.

The test approach should include exit criteria or, in Agile organizations, definitions of done. What would constitute "ready for delivery" in terms of the app? What constitutes "done" in terms of testing, completeness of the testing work? It's a common practice for testing to end once you've run out of time, provided no one is aware of any show stoppers, but that's pretty weak. Such an exit criterion should only be used for apps where quality doesn't matter, and, in that case, why is your organization bothering to test it at all?

The test approach should also discuss the type of test methods and tools you'll use and the different quality characteristics you are concerned with. We will return to these topics in Chapters 3 and 4.

Another part of your test approach relates to test documentation. How detailed will your test plan be, and why? For example, in a fast-paced life cycle, you probably won't have time to write a 30-page test plan, but what does need to be documented? Are there regulations that affect your documentation, such as those that apply to regulated medical, avionics, or other safety-critical apps? Are you working with a distributed test team and do you need to communicate across time zones?

2.4 Test your knowledge

Let's try one or more sample exam questions related to the material we've just covered. The answers are found in Appendix C.

Question 5 Learning objective: recall of syllabus content only (K1)

In which of the following ways do risks to application quality affect the test approach?

 A. prioritization of testing;
 B. evaluation of pass/fail status of a test;
 C. contingency planning for staff turnover;
 D. accessibility testing.

5 IDENTIFY TEST CONDITIONS AND SET SCOPE

The learning objective for Chapter 2, Section 5, is as follows:

MOB-2.5.1 (K2) Describe how test analysts should take the device and application into consideration when creating test conditions.

With our coverage goals set and the test approach, and our means to achieve those goals defined, we are ready to get specific about the test conditions. Test conditions is another ISTQB® phrase, which, simply put, means **what to test**, or **the list of stuff you will cover with your tests**. The ISTQB® distinguishes between test conditions—**what to test**—and test cases—which are **how to test**.

Test analysis is the process that identifies the test conditions, and it comprises many of the activities we've been discussing so far. Test design is the process that elaborates test conditions into test cases, at some appropriate level of detail. Whatever that level of detail is, and however test conditions and test cases will be documented, you should explain this in your test approach, so people have clear expectations about the test documentation.

An example of a test condition might be (if you are testing an ecommerce application), **test successful purchases with all supported credit cards**. It says what to test, but it doesn't say how to test it. That said, a clever and experienced tester might very well be able to figure out, based on such test conditions alone, how to do the testing. Well, if that's true, you and your colleagues are clever and experienced. You don't need any further guidance to tell you how to test those conditions.

Further, suppose there is no regulatory requirement for you to document the tests in any more detail. In that case, you might decide not to document test cases, but rather just the test conditions. Obviously, there's a significant skills consideration here. Do you and your fellow testers have the competence to design test cases on the fly, while executing the tests, without anything documented beyond the test conditions? Or will you—or maybe some of the other testers—need more detail, in the form of logical test cases or even concrete test cases?

Whatever level of documentation your test cases will have—none, some, a lot—you need to map your risk analysis to your test conditions, so that you have clear guidance regarding how much time to spend creating and executing the test cases. Remember, in the section on risk analysis, I mentioned my article, "Matching Test Techniques to the Extent of Testing," which explains which techniques to use based on the level of risk. This is the point where that guidance becomes important, because, without clear guidance, you will over-test some conditions and under-test others.

Now, it might be that you and your fellow testers don't need detailed test cases in advance, but you do want to be specific about your test conditions. This can be especially useful if you want to capture details of your test cases as you run them. To return to our example, instead of a test condition that simply says, **complete a purchase with each supported credit card**, you might have four specific test conditions:

- complete a purchase with American Express®;

- complete a purchase with Discover;
- complete a purchase with Visa;
- complete a purchase with MasterCard®.

I have four test conditions, one for each supported card. It's clear what the supported cards are, so we won't miss any. Further, when I run the tests, if any one test fails, I know specifically which credit card is not working. I can also use a simple text capture tool, or a more sophisticated tool such as Rapid Reporter, to capture the specific steps, the specific inputs, and the specific results.[12]

Some of my clients who use such tools then load the post hoc test cases into a test management tool and establish traceability, thus having the benefits of a fully documented set of tests. The downside of this post hoc approach to documenting tests is that you're taking time away from test execution to document the tests. That could reduce the overall extent of testing that you can do, so consider the tradeoff.

In some cases, assuming you do document them, you might be better off writing the test cases before you start test execution. I've had testers in certain Agile teams tell me, "The first half of the sprint is pretty slow for us. The developers tend to create these large user stories. They don't have anything for us to test until halfway through the sprint, but then we're hellishly busy, because all the content of the sprint starts raining down on us for the rest of the sprint." If this is your life, and you need to have documented test cases, you might want to spend time documenting the test cases early in the sprint rather than documenting the test cases as they're being run.

Remember that, in risk-based testing, you want to run your tests in risk order, so that you find the scary bugs early. So, whether you run directly from test conditions or use test cases, you'll need them prioritized based on risk. When you start test execution, you want to start with the most important tests.

It might be that you get to a point where you run out of time. In risk-based testing, the test conditions you haven't covered should be relatively low risk, compared to the ones you did cover. This is not an ideal situation, though. It's better if you look at ways to cover your lower-risk test conditions opportunistically, as part of testing other test conditions. To use a trivial example, if authenticating user names and passwords is considered low risk, that's obviously something that we can easily test as part of testing something else.

Even if the test cases aren't documented, the test conditions should be documented, at the appropriate level of detail, so that they can be reviewed by your business and technical stakeholders. It is also important that, when you capture those test conditions in your test management tool, whatever it is, you capture traceability information. This way, the test conditions trace back to the various dimensions of test coverage that we talked about earlier, such as user stories, risks, supported configurations, and the like. When the test conditions can be tracked back to specific coverage items, this allows you to report your test results in terms of risk mitigation. For example, suppose you have this risk, **app accepts credit card transactions that should be rejected**. Suppose there are four tests associated with that risk. If all four of those tests pass, we can say that

---

[12] You can find information about Rapid Reporter at: http://testing.gershon.info/reporter/

risk has been mitigated. If, instead, three out of the four tests have been run and those tests pass, but there's one test left to be run, the risk is not fully mitigated yet, because there's still stuff we don't know.

Now, let's say you've run all four tests and two out of the four tests have failed. Here again, the risk is not mitigated, because we have at least two known problems. That said, the risk is reduced, because those bugs can be fixed and the tests rerun. Now, if the tests pass, then that risk is fully mitigated. As you can see, when you can talk about conditions that pass and don't pass, you can talk about risks that are mitigated and not mitigated. This makes test results fully transparent to your non-tester stakeholders.

All too often, we testers make the mistake of reporting test results as follows: "We ran 262 tests; 198 of them passed. Thirty of them failed. The rest are yet to be run. We found 96 bugs. Of those, 87 have been fixed. The remainder are still open."

Non-testers listen to those kinds of test status reports totally mystified. They are thinking, if not saying, "What does that mean? Are we done? Are we almost done? Does the app suck or is it almost ready for users?"

However, when you start talking about risks that are not mitigated and risks that are mitigated, test conditions that work and don't work, people get that. That allows them to make smart decisions about releases, project status, and so forth.

When you're creating your test conditions, remember the physical stuff, remember the functional stuff, and remember the non-functional stuff. The non-functional stuff is easy to forget. The physical stuff is what makes testing a mobile app different than testing a PC application.[13]

As discussed before, let risk be your guide in terms of how much testing you do in these different areas. It's very easy to get distracted by the bright shiny object, leading to people spending too much time testing things that are actually not high risk. The approach to risk analysis discussed earlier will allow you to then think about your test conditions in these physical, functional and non-functional areas, and come up with the specific test conditions you need to cover, together with the breadth and depth of coverage that is necessary for each one of those conditions.

It is important that you go through this process of analysis, carefully deciding what to test. It can be tempting to go looking for some universal list of test conditions that must be covered for mobile apps. If such a list does exist out on the vast internet, it is the brainchild of a fool. While you can use ideas from the internet to help you come up with good test conditions, it is by following proven best practices of test analysis that you'll get the right list.

To illustrate this concept, let's return to the senior personal health app example. Here's an example of a physical test condition: **gathering heart rate sensor information when available**. If the phone has a built-in heart rate sensor, or it connects via Bluetooth to

---

[13] You can find more information on how physical factors affect mobile apps here: https://rbcs-us.com/resources/webinars/webinar-the-more-things-change-location-the-more-they-stay-the-same-9-22-2017/

something that does heart rate sensing, the app should use that information, and this test condition says we should test that.

Here's another example of a physical test condition: **saving the location of the user when sensor data is gathered or when the user enters data**. Any time sensor data, such as heart rate data, is captured or the user makes an entry, the app should use the geolocation sensor to determine where the user currently is and save that information along with the sensor or input data. This test condition says we should test that.

Here's an example of a functional test condition: **charting weight, body mass index, blood pressure, and resting heart rate over time**.

Here's an example of a non-functional test condition: **encryption of the patient data using a strong key that's unique to each user**. This way, even if somebody manages to crack into one of the patient's datasets, it doesn't mean that the hacker would be able to get into all of them.

Now, obviously, those are not the only four test conditions for this app, but those are four in each of the three areas.

2.5 Test your knowledge

Let's try one or more sample exam questions related to the material we've just covered. The answers are found in Appendix C.

Question 6 Learning objective: MOB-2.5.1 (K2) Describe how test analysts should take the device and application into consideration when creating test conditions

Which of the following is a test condition that is related to the physical capabilities of a device?

    A.   Enter a first and last name; click create account; verify account.
    B.   Check app acceptance of valid credit.
    C.   Verify app ability to locate nearest petrol station.
    D.   Verify app ability to resume downloads on reconnect.

6 REGRESSION TESTING

The learning objective for Chapter 2, Section 6, is recall of syllabus content only.

It's a hassle, but you must consider regression tests. Stuff changes. Firmware changes, often without any notice. Devices change, though at least you'll have a way to know when they do. Interoperating software changes, probably without any easy way to know it did without doing some research. Network providers make changes, and they probably won't bother to warn you. Connectivity protocols can change. People can start using your app in new locations. Entirely new devices come out, or new sensors are added to existing devices.

One mobile testing course attendee mentioned a situation where their app did not change, but they had to support a new version of a browser. This required lots of regression testing. This is a potential risk of using the mobile-optimized website or hybrid app approach to going mobile, rather than a native app. If your app is accessed through a browser, you're tied to the vendor of that browser.

That's also true if your native app uses any other app on the device. If that app changes, it could break your app. This is compounded by the fact that there's no implied warranty of fitness or any other sort of guarantee associated with software, as exists for most physical products. Instead, we have these ridiculous click-through agreements that basically say a vendor can change their software any time they want, and, if by so doing, they burn your house down, effectively, they have no responsibility for the consequences, even if they were negligent in their testing of their own app. This allows software companies to completely shift the external costs of failure onto their customers and end users, unless you hold them accountable through one-star reviews and the like. Until software engineering matures a lot more as a profession, expect to need to do a lot of externally triggered regression testing.

You **are** probably updating your app frequently, because that's common practice with mobile apps. Even if you're not updating your app frequently, you're going to regression test frequently, because every single hour of every single day somebody else is changing something that could break your app. So keep track of what's changing out there that could affect your app, and regression test accordingly.

Given the frequency of regression testing, and the number of regression tests you might need, you probably should look at some approach for automation. We will cover that later in this book. Not only do these automated regression tests require care and feeding, remember that your test environments must be kept current, too. Be careful that your simulators are up to date as well.

2.6 Test your knowledge

Let's try one or more sample exam questions related to the material we've just covered. The answers are found in Appendix C.

Question 7 Learning objective: recall of syllabus content only (K1)

Which of the following statements is true?

    A. Mobile regression tests cannot be automated.
    B. Regression risk is lower for mobile applications.
    C. Regression testing can be necessary even if the application doesn't change.
    D. Regression testing can be done entirely with simulators.

In this chapter, you've seen ways to determine what to test, and how to test those things. You considered how to identify the functions and attributes your app has, and how those functions and attributes could fail. You saw that there are strategies to help you achieve the right balancing act between testing too much and testing too little. You've seen how to define a test approach that focuses you on the important test conditions and keeps the testing effort within scope. Finally, you've considered the important topic of regression testing.

3 QUALITY CHARACTERISTICS FOR MOBILE TESTING

In this important chapter, we will address the important ways in which test design and implementation differ for mobile apps. We will start by examining functional testing, looking at security, interoperability, compatibility, accuracy, and suitability. We'll discuss various traditional and untraditional techniques for creating functional mobile tests. Next, we move on to non-functional testing, specifically performance, usability, reliability, and portability.

CHAPTER SECTIONS

Chapter 3, Quality Characteristics for Mobile Testing, contains the following three sections:

1. Introduction
2. Functional testing
3. Non-functional testing

CHAPTER TERMS

The terms to remember for Chapter 3 are as follows:

- geolocation;
- TestStorming,

1 INTRODUCTION

The learning objective for Chapter 3, Section 1, is recall of syllabus content only.

Here in Chapter 3, we are going to talk about functional and non-functional quality characteristics. These are the attributes that bear on what the software does—its functions—and how it does what it does—its non-functional behavior while it carries out those functions. We use that as a point of departure to talk about how to test those functional and non-functional quality characteristics, specifically as they relate to mobile apps.

Let's start by clarifying functional testing and non-functional testing. One way to think of this is grammatically. Consider an ATM. What does an ATM let you do? It lets you withdraw cash, make deposits, do balance inquiries, and transfer funds. Grammatically, those are all verb phrases. Withdraw cash. Make deposits. Do balance inquiries. Transfer funds. There's a verb and a noun there, forming a verb phrase.

Now, think about how we want the ATM to do what it does. Quickly. Reliably. Easily. Those are adverbs. So, if you're thinking about a system and you're thinking about what it does, the verb phrases, that's the functional piece. If you're thinking about how it does it, the adverbs and adjectives, that's the non-functional piece.

It's important to keep in mind that there is no magic list of quality characteristics that are applicable to all apps, or of equal importance for all apps. As I mentioned earlier, security is a big issue for a banking app, whereas if you have an app that allows you play solitaire, there's really not a security risk present.

3.1 Test your knowledge

Let's try one or more sample exam questions related to the material we've just covered. The answers are found in Appendix C.

Question 1 Learning objective: term understanding (K1)

What is geolocation?

    A.   A pointer that references a location that is out of scope for that pointer or that does not exist.

    B.   The identification of the real-world geographical location of a device.

    C.   A data item that specifies the location of another data item.

    D.   A piece of data embedded in a digital media file to indicate geographical information about the subject, usually latitude and longitude.

2 FUNCTIONAL TESTING

The learning objectives for Chapter 3, Section 2, are as follows:

MOB-3.2.1   (K3) For a given mobile testing project apply the appropriate test design techniques.

MOB-3.2.2   (K1) Recall the purpose of testing for the correctness of an application.

MOB-3.2.3   (K2) Explain the important considerations for planning security testing for a mobile application.

MOB-3.2.4 (K2) Summarize the concepts of perspectives and personas for use in mobile application testing.

MOB-3.2.5 (K2) Summarize how device differences may affect testing.

MOB-3.2.6 (K2) Explain the use of TestStorming for deriving test conditions.

Note that one of these learning objectives—"MOB-3.2.1 (K3) For a given mobile testing project apply the appropriate test design techniques"—relates to the test design techniques described in the ISTQB® Certified Tester Foundation syllabus 2018 in Chapter 4. You should read this section of the syllabus if you're not familiar with it, or it's been a long time since you went through it.[1]

In addition, you should be able to apply those techniques with K3 learning objectives defined for them in Chapter 4 of the ISTQB® Certified Tester Foundation syllabus 2018. K3-level questions related to those techniques can appear in the ASTQB Certified Mobile Tester exam. Try some reputable Foundation-level test design sample questions, such as those provided by RBCS, as part of preparing for the mobile exam.[2]

Functional testing is about what the application does. It's focused on four main characteristics:

- accuracy;
- suitability;
- security;
- interoperability.

Let's examine testing for each of these functional quality characteristics.

Accuracy testing checks whether the app actually gives you the right answer. One accuracy test for an ecommerce application, for example, would check for incorrect calculation of shipping charges.

Suitability testing checks whether the app delivers the features that it was supposed to deliver. An application can work accurately yet not be suitable, because it does not have the features to do something that you need to do. One suitability test for an airline app, for example, would check that it that allows you not only to search for flights, but to complete the booking of the flight once you've found it.

Security testing checks whether the app can deny unauthorized access to data and features, while at the same time allowing authorized access to data and features. One

---

[1] You can read the syllabus here: https://certifications.bcs.org/upload/pdf/swt-foundation-syllabus.pdf
[2] You can find ISTQB® Foundation training options and resources, and other training options and resources, on our website, www.rbcs-us.com

security test for a pharmacy app, for example, would make sure that each customer could access their own prescription data, but not any other customer's prescription data.

Interoperability testing checks whether the app works properly with other apps that it uses or that use it. One interoperability test for a restaurant-locating app, for example, would make sure that you can click on a restaurant's phone number and that this action will correctly result in the phone app dialing the restaurant's given phone number.

Testing of accuracy and suitability are what most testers think of when they think of doing functional testing. In addition, the topics of testing accuracy and suitability are covered in the ISTQB® Certified Tester Foundation syllabus 2018, in Chapter 4. So, you should already be familiar with testing of accuracy and suitability, from either having taken that exam, or from reading that chapter in the syllabus as suggested at the beginning of this section. Further, the testing of accuracy and suitability on mobile apps does not differ significantly from testing these characteristics on other kinds of software.

However, interoperability and security testing are not addressed in any depth in the ISTQB® Foundation syllabus 2018. In addition, both testing of security and interoperability can be significantly different for mobile apps compared to other kinds of software. So, in the next subsections, let's look at these two characteristics in more detail, and how we should test them.

Security

Security testing is particularly important these days, for many applications. While it's a specialized field of expertise, you should at least be aware of the basics. If you decide to become a security expert, there's a lot to learn here, and a good career can be had in this field.

After you finish the ASTQB Mobile Tester certification, a next step to become even more security aware, and indeed able to do security testing, is to study for and pass the ISTQB® Advanced Security Tester certification.[3] The Advanced Security Tester exam is more complicated than the mobile testing exam, more along the lines of the Advanced Technical Test Analyst exam in terms of the level of difficulty.

> Over a decade ago, I took my first security certification exam, the CompTIA Security+ exam. One thing I remember from studying for that exam was that of all the tools that are available, many of them are free. Many of those tools have funny names like SATAN and its successor, SAINT. However, these tools are sophisticated. You must have the skills to interpret what the tools are telling you and the skills to be able to use the tool properly.

So, while you won't become a security testing expert in the next few minutes, I can make you security aware. The first thing to be aware of is that security bugs, unlike most other bugs, tend to be passive rather than active. What I mean by security bugs being passive is that someone—either a hacker, a criminal, a disgruntled worker or a security

---

[3] See www.istqb.org/downloads/category/46-advanced-level-security-tester.html

tester—must try to exploit the bugs in order for the security failure to occur. Contrast that to a simple accuracy bug, which will give the wrong answer to anyone, regardless of an intention to cause a failure. Therefore, it's important to think of ways in which security risks can exist, so that you can test for them. Let's look at some of these risks.

First, mobile apps often are accessing information across networks, which can involve sending and receiving information over public Wi-Fi networks. Such public networks are inherently risky, as it's easy for criminals to monitor traffic on them. Therefore, any sensitive data sent to or from your app needs to be encrypted.

The mobile device itself is subject to attack because people will download and install apps without asking an obvious question: "Who created this app?" Now, most people, when using their PCs, know that they shouldn't open an attachment sent by somebody they don't know, but the same people will download and install apps created by people they don't know. Any such app could conceivably be a Trojan Horse.

Further, people don't always set up good security on their mobile devices—or their PCs for that matter. The difference is that people don't tend to carry PCs around and lose them in public places. I travel a lot, and I can tell you that one of the most common public announcements in an airport has to do with asking a person—by name, mind you—to come back to the security checkpoint to claim their phone. A lost, unsecured phone can mean giving up whatever information—including private and confidential information— to whoever finds it.

Similarly, when people surrender their devices, they might or might not wipe the data from them first. For example, when people trade in a phone for another phone, they might be too excited about the new phone to remember to wipe the old one, so there could be private and confidential information left on it. Even if it's wiped, you have to ask, "What's the level of security of that wipe?" Just deleting something is not enough and just overwriting a memory location once is typically not enough to make it impossible to un-erase.

Mobile apps also pose a particular challenge in that they sometimes use many different communication channels. Some of these are inherently insecure, or easy to use in an insecure way. For most PCs and laptops, the only inherently insecure channel is Wi-Fi. However, mobile apps use channels in addition to Wi-Fi that can be insecure.

For example, suppose you're texting with somebody via SMS. That's insecure, as your network carrier has access to those messages. Now, a security-aware person would say, "No, I never do that. I use the Telegram app." Okay, but are you using it properly? By default, if you start a chat with somebody in Telegram it's not secure. You have to start an encrypted chat, and, when you start the chat, tell the app to have the thread self-destruct when you end the chat, for the messages to be truly secure.

So, just because somebody's using software that has security in it doesn't mean they're using it in a way which is secure. For example, plenty of people use passwords that are ridiculously short or obvious.

As you become more security aware, something to keep in mind is that almost all of your app's users will not have that same security mindset. More than anything else, my first security certification over a decade ago, for the Security Plus exam, flipped a switch in my head that hadn't been on before. It made me look at the world in a different way. That's become even truer since I got the ISTQB® Advanced Security Tester certification. I've become constantly aware of security when thinking about software and systems. I now consider the implications of security, and the complexity of security.

I find I have a much better understanding now when I hear security and privacy issues being talked about in the news and by my clients. I can recognize when somebody doesn't understand security, its implications, and its limitations, especially when I hear them suggesting something that's simply not possible.

This awareness is a valuable thing. However, remember, even though you've had that switch turned on your head, maybe by taking some courses on security testing or security, your users have not. Those users might do things that, when you hear about them, make you think, "Why on earth would you do that?" The answer is simple: because they don't think about security.

It's not just the users who can be security unsavvy. Developers can be sometimes, too. So, when testing an app, look for situations where sensitive information is being stored on the device or stored in the app.

Finally, you might want to consider how your app behaves on an iPhone after jailbreaking, or an Android phone after rooting, or another model of phone after the equivalent modification. That will potentially change the security behavior of your app. Now, your managers may say, "Hey, people aren't supposed to do that, and that's not supported by the device vendors, so why should we worry about what happens?" I guess the answer to this question would depend on the risk associated with your app having a security breach.

Let's look at an open-source repository of ideas for security testing: OWASP.

OWASP

Now, OWASP is not something you say right before a flying insect stings you—though I usually say something a little stronger than that! OWASP is the Open Web Application Security Project, and their website is a treasure-trove for the security minded—and yes it has a little wasp icon on it.

OWASP is an open-source volunteer organization, similar to the volunteer organizations that create and maintain tools like JUnit and Selenium. However, OWASP focuses on creating security-related resources, and not so much tools, but information.[4] On the OWASP website, one resource available is a list of major mobile app security risks.[5] Let's review some of these mobile app security risks here.

---

[4] Unlike some sites, owasp.org is vendor neutral. So, it's not a marketing tool for a security tool vendor or a security consulting company. Sure, there's valid security-related information available from security tool vendors and security consulting companies, but you can count on that information being self-serving. After all, my company, RBCS, provides all sorts of free testing-related resources on our website, including well over 250 hours of free information about software testing in the form of videos, recorded webinars, articles, and more. Ultimately, though, we want you to come to our website and buy services from us, and we certainly don't include information that would tend to steer you towards our competitors.

[5] You can find the latest version of the list here: www.owasp.org/index.php/Projects/OWASP_Mobile_Security_Project_-_Top_Ten_Mobile_Risks

- Weak server-side controls: an example of this occurs when the server-side trusts the authentication via the native app or hybrid app. For example, if a native app establishes a connection to the server, the server-side software might assume that the user is who the app claims it is. This could be easily defeated on the device side, or bypassed by talking directly to the interface the server presents to the wider world.

- Insecure data storage on the device or the server-side: this is another major risk. Devices get lost, as I mentioned before, and servers get hacked.

- Insecure data transfer: examples of problems here include improper or weak encryption of private identifying information or not using secure protocols like HTTPS or FTPS when you should or using those channels in a way that's weak.

- Accidental data leakage: an example of this is having to decrypt encrypted data in order to use it—suppose we store private information about a user's medical history on a device, and we allow the user to add, modify, and delete information. The information must be decrypted to be shown to the user. If that information is stored in a temporary location, and the temporary location is accessible, it could result in data leakage, again on the server-side or the client-side.

- Weak authentication and authorization: authentication problems can result in a situation where the person using the mobile app is not really the person that we think is using the mobile app. It's actually some other person who managed to get a hold of that person's credentials. Authorization problems can result in a person being able to access functions and data they really shouldn't have access to, or retaining access after that access has been revoked or expired.

- Encryption failures: an example problem here is that the use of weaker encryption algorithms, possibly for purposes of backwards-compatibility or speed, make an application vulnerable. Even strong algorithms can be made weak by the use of poor passwords.

- Client-side injection: this is when an attacker forces or tricks an application into using data that is especially designed to hijack the application itself. This can be for purposes of, say, uploading personal identifying information from the device to some target data repository on the internet, using the app as the unwitting tool of exploitation.

- Invalid security decisions via untrusted inputs: these can occur when your app has interfaces which are accessible to other apps. If attackers can figure out how to exploit those interfaces, they can force your app to carry out an action or divulge sensitive information without the user having any way of knowing this has happened. Such an attack could occur using a Trojan Horse-type downloaded app, for example.

- Improper session handling: much of the internet runs on what are called stateless protocols such as SOAP and HTTP. However, people carry out sensitive activities through a process of authenticating and receiving authorization, which requires a notion of a state. State information can be handled via cookies or other tokens, for example, but such cookies and other tokens can, if not handled securely, leak to an attacker, thus allowing the attacker to carry out actions as if they were authenticated.

- Lack of binary protection: this can occur when someone gets the binary of your app and manages to reverse-engineer the source code from it. This could be for purposes of stealing an algorithm, producing a knock-off of your app, or for figuring out how to access sensitive information used by your app.

Further security testing considerations

As I've said, there's lots to consider when doing security testing, but let's review some common areas to cover.

First, when security testing an application, make sure that the right people and the right applications can access the functionality and data they're authorized to access. Conversely, make sure that people and applications that should not access certain functionality and data can't do so. It's the latter half of that statement which is more complex and requires more thought and more work. It's possible to list, from an analysis of role-based security, what it means for the right people and the right applications to get access to the things they should get access to, and that list can be used as a set of test conditions. However, it's much harder to identify all the interesting test conditions related to checking for the wrong people or apps getting access to things that they shouldn't get access to.

Access to data doesn't only occur through the app itself. The data must be stored and retrieved in between the time it's being accessed, which would be most of the time for most data. So, when the data is stored, at the very least the sensitive data should be encrypted, and encrypted in a strong, secure way. When the data is in transit, regardless of the protocol being used, again at the very least, the sensitive data should be securely encrypted. While the obvious consideration here is the cellular or Wi-Fi network, don't forget data flowing between the mobile device and devices attached to it, such as Bluetooth keyboards. Your app should not send sensitive data in the clear—that is, unencrypted—under any circumstances.

Finally, if you are involved in testing in-house apps, make sure to test whether security policies are followed correctly for all mobile devices, including people's own devices if they brought them to work. There are plenty of corporate horror stories that start with people losing devices that weren't properly secured and had company information on them.

Now, how far you go with this security testing depends on how important security is for your application. If you're working on a game of solitaire, there's not a whole lot of security risk there. If you're writing an app that accesses bank accounts, that's totally different.

Figure 3.1 shows the Paloma app running on a Windows device. To log in, you use a frequent flyer number and a password. Now, obviously, the app must ensure that the person is who they say they are in order to check in or book a flight.

However, if someone is just checking flight status, do they have to be logged in? No, such a user should be able to do it as a guest. There's nothing personal about that. Checking bag rules, likewise, doesn't involve personal information, so a guest should be able to do it.

Figure 3.1 Home screen for an airline app

Notice that there's another difference here. Accessing flight status information requires a network connection, while bag rules might not, once downloaded.

If the user books a flight, the app communicates to the server-side, so that transaction must be secure on both the client-side and the server-side. The client-side security can be tested through the user interface (UI) on the device. However, for the server-side, you'll need some technical folks to help you with that, unless you already know the interfaces between the app on the device and the server, plus the data flows once the data gets to the initial server. Just because the data is transferred securely from the device to the web server or other initial point of contact doesn't mean that insecure handling subsequently won't create an issue.

Interoperability and compatibility

Another consideration from a functional point of view is interoperability, which is sometimes called compatibility, though those are subtly different, as I'll describe below. Interoperability is a big deal on mobile devices, because many apps use other apps to do something, thus avoiding the need to build that functionality into the app itself.

For example, consider Facebook. I can directly access the camera app via the Facebook mobile app to take a picture and embed that picture into a post. That's a form of interoperability, which we can think of as basic local interoperability. There's also interoperability with server components, which happens when the mobile app talks across the network to an interface on the server-side.

Both local and remote interoperability can occur, too. Suppose I use Yelp to find a restaurant, then click on the address for the restaurant. Yelp invokes the map app on the device, and passes the address to that app. Unless the map for the current location is already downloaded, the map app may then use the network to contact its designated online map repository. From a test point of view, notice that this is a single use case for the user, but failure can occur at any point along the way.

If there are apps outside your control that are new or changing, this creates some test challenges, too. For example, if Google changes the default Android camera app on my phone, such a change could potentially break the Facebook feature that allows me to insert pictures directly into a post.

> That kind of stuff does get broken during updates. My Android phone auto-updated its operating system at one point, despite the fact that I asked it twice not to do so. It went ahead and updated the phone anyway. That caused a whole bunch of stuff not to work. For example, when the phone was first updated, most of the contact information was missing. However—and this was really weird—the contact information magically came back the next day. Where did it go? Why did it come back? I don't know. Most of the stuff that was rendered inoperable, though, such as Facebook, Twitter, and a number of other apps, had to be uninstalled and reinstalled.

While interoperability is sometimes called compatibility, there's actually a difference. Interoperability involves an active conversation going on between apps or components, where one uses the other to get a specific thing done. The conversation can be seen as horizontal. Compatibility is more vertical. Alternatively, it's possible to think of compatibility as a special form of interoperability that looks at how your app interoperates with the components provided by the device, the operating system, and similar inherent capabilities of the mobile device hosting your app.

For example, if your app runs in a browser, or otherwise uses a browser, compatibility testing starts with identifying the different browsers your app supports. With some browser-based apps, and especially native apps, you have to identify the different supported devices and the different ways those devices can be configured. You also have to be ready to test changes that occur, whether your app changed or not.

It's also important to remember that interoperability and compatibility exist in a dynamic setting. As one reviewer of this book wrote,

> [There are important] test conditions related to inter-dependencies and [it's important to] combine those test conditions. The conditions I'm thinking about are charging the device, using the device, communicating data with the device and the app [while checking that] nothing goes wrong with that data, [then combine those with] a 'receipt of notifications' test condition. This is a critical part of mobile app testing. [Testers must] understand the inter-dependencies within the app. I suggest testers work closely with developers to understand where and when those inter-dependencies come into play. The thinking tester can then figure out how better to create specific tests appropriate for their user base.

For compatibility and interoperability, you should use risk-based testing to figure out where to focus. You can use equivalence partitioning to recognize different, relevant options for each of the factors that are involved. If the risk is high enough, you might consider combinatorial testing, at least for those factors you worry will interfere with each other.

If your app is already in operation, you should have some logs. You can apply some analytics to help you figure out what your user base looks like, what different configurations are in use, and so forth.

Variability

If you're new to testing mobile apps, it can come as a surprise that mobile devices differ in ways that a typical PC might not. Usually PCs differ primarily in terms of memory size, disk space, and CPU power. Mobile devices compete not just on those three dimensions, but also other factors such as screen size, screen resolution, battery life, the different kinds of input devices and sensors present in the device itself or supported by the device, and other factors. These factors can interact with each other. For example, a faster CPU accessing more memory will drain power from a battery faster, and one of the reviewers of this book mentioned seeing fast device chargers wreaking havoc with an app's data or functionality. As I've said previously, if your app has a number of mobile devices to support, that factor has some potentially costly testing implications.

Another dimension of variability is the connection. There are different network providers with their data plans and data limits, which can potentially affect the way your app works or can be used. Furthermore, mobile devices, naturally enough, move around. This affects the quality, speed, and type of connection, so that's something else you have to take into account from a testing point of view.

Mobile devices often support external peripherals, which might be used by your app or affect the way your app works. For example, for my phone I have a little USB to HDMI converter. It's really cool conceptually, as it allows you to connect to a HDMI monitor or flat-screen TV and project your screen onto the HDMI device. Unfortunately, it doesn't work very well. It's very picky about which HDMI port you connect to, and the order in which you make the physical connection. It's too bad, because I spend a lot of time in hotels, which usually have HDMI-enabled TVs. My plan was to use my phone for streaming movies and as a pseudo-desktop to read email with a full-sized screen. Sadly, because it doesn't work very well, I almost never use it.

As a person involved in app testing, you should identify—via equivalence partitioning, not brute force listing of all models—these different external peripherals that are supported on the devices you support. These peripherals could include Bluetooth keyboards, headphones, speakers, HDMI video adapters, credit card readers, and more. With these peripherals, you should determine whether some of your users might use one of those peripherals with your app. If so, then there's a risk-based decision you need to make about whether you should test that peripheral–device combination.

When you do your equivalence partitioning of devices and peripherals, be careful not to group together items that actually behave differently in ways that are relevant to your app. For example, one Android phone can be different to another Android phone. Some of the large Android phone vendors compete fiercely, and they do so by trying to differentiate their version of an Android phone from their competitors. So, if you just test your app and the supported peripherals on a single model of Android phone, there could be some differences.

Even within a single model of phone, there can be differences with connectivity, security, interoperability with similar devices, how sensor data is made available to the apps, and so forth. For example, I choose to put the largest possible SD card in my phones, because I listen to lots of podcasts and music. This means my phone has a somewhat different configuration than most other people's phones. I had a phone which had problems any time I rebooted the system with content on the SD card. I suspect that I simply overwhelmed the phone with this huge SD card with lots of content.

Say, for example, your app can access data on an SD card. You plug in a small SD card, put a few files on it, and open one of those files. That doesn't cover my user profile. To cover my user profile, take the largest supported SD card, copy MP3s, MP4s, PNGs, JPEGs and so forth to the card until it's almost full, and then copy some files that your app uses onto that SD card. See if your app can find and open those files. See if your app can do so immediately after the phone has been rebooted. As one reviewer of the book wrote,

> Knowing the limitations of your app on a particular device is [an important] test [including for] updates. Knowing thresholds, limitations, and how the app handles those limitations is important information a tester can share with the project team.

The variety of devices, the variety of physical and functional abilities offered by those devices and the peripherals available for those devices will probably continue to get more complicated and more diverse. In part, consumer demand drives this push away from homogeneity, but the vendors are responsible, too. While I don't have access to the secret strategies of Samsung, Apple, LG and other phone manufacturers, I'm sure they recognize what happened to the PC business when PCs became fully commoditized in the late 1990s and early 2000s, with laptops close behind. It's not good to be a vendor in a commodity market, because economics says you don't make much money on commodities.[6]

---

[6] Think about rice for example. Certainly, there are some companies that sell boutique types of rice, but for the most part, when somebody's looking for a bag of rice, they go into the store and buy the cheapest bag of long grain white rice they can find. The competition in commodity markets is on price, not features. Further, quality is a given in a commodity market, and, if you fail to deliver consistent quality, you're dead in that market.

Device differentiation and its effect on testing

Phone vendors certainly don't want commoditization. One way to forestall that is to constantly introduce new features on their phones that nobody else has—at least until they catch up, but by that time you've introduced two or three other features in your next version. That features arms race shows no sign of slowing down.

Another way vendors stave off commoditization is through what's called **the walled garden**. This is done by building a family of devices that all interoperate with each other and share common proprietary features, and work much less well with other brands. Apple is the great example of this approach. They try to bewitch you with all the wonderful features inside their walled garden, and they have been quite successful.

Other vendors try to do the same thing. For example, my LG phone has certain features that will work with LG video devices using a proprietary communication channel. To avoid commoditization, the vendors want to create a set of features and capabilities that are unique to their brand family. Even if another vendor has that same set of capabilities, if it's not accessible from one vendor to the other, it's a classic software thing: vendor lock-in.

> Now, to be fair, automakers would do that same thing, if only they could. If Ford, Toyota, Mercedes, and the other automakers could figure out a way of forcing you to buy branded gas that they could sell at a premium, which would work in their cars and only their cars, they would do it in a heartbeat. Vendor lock-in is not a particular evil that exists in the hearts only of tech companies. All companies want captive customers because companies with captive customers don't face as much competition, thanks to what are called barriers to exit.

Let's look at an example of the intersection between device support and testing. When I got a new brand of smartphone a number of years ago, I configured it so that I could send and receive email from it.[7]

I found this worked well, to the point where I decided I wanted to respond to many of my emails on my phone. To type longer responses, though, I would need a Bluetooth keyboard. Well, to my unhappy surprise, I discovered that my brand of smartphone did not support Bluetooth keyboards.

So, when it was time for a new phone, Bluetooth keyboard support was a major consideration. I've got a keyboard now that connects with my Android phone and with my Kindle Fire. On either platform, using that keyboard, I can handle emails almost as if I were working on my laptop.

I was at a conference recently where I didn't even bother to bring my PC, which I'd have to lock to a table to be sure it wouldn't get stolen. Instead, I just slipped my phone, my

---

[7] I hadn't done that with my previous phone, an iPhone, just because I was worried that more time spent reading email would only lead to more email. When I got this particular brand of smartphone, I decided to try it, since I could use downtime such as when I'm at the gym to clean up my junk email and respond quickly to urgent email.

Bluetooth keyboard and a charger into my suit pocket. I was able to handle all my email processing for the day.

So, let's say that you're creating something like Google Docs or some other app that supports heavy text editing. If you have one phone that supports Bluetooth keyboards and another that does not, which one of these would you recommend supporting? Unless there are strong market reasons to support the non-Bluetooth phone, why set your users up for frustration?

If you do have to support both, there will clearly be differences in the way the functionality works. Obviously, your app's users can write a lengthy document if they have a Bluetooth keyboard available on their device. So, you should consider that when you create your tests. You should also consider the usability of your app on each device, which is affected by the supported peripheral—in this case the keyboard—as well. Certainly, from a test results comparison point of view, these are different types of tests, so consider how you compare the results.

Test design: using the classic techniques

Having reviewed functionality, let's see how that relates to test design. During test design, you have to consider your app's functionality, supported device functionality and how those two intersect. Remember, too, that there's the device functionality that your app uses and there's the device functionality that your app doesn't use, which might interact with your app in some way. Suppose you have an app that plays music, such as a single-user game that plays background music whilst you're playing the game. It would probably work with a Bluetooth headphone or other audio device, but how about the cellular network? At first you might say, "No, there really shouldn't be any interaction there," but what happens when a phone call occurs while you're in the middle of playing a game with background music playing? If you answer the call, you need to pause the game, which includes pausing the music. I've found some situations with my phone where it doesn't always properly do that. If I'm using an app that uses audio features and I answer the phone, the audio continues to play. So clearly something didn't get tested properly.

One reviewer of this book stressed the importance of this kind of notification-interruption testing, writing,

> How are those notifications sent to the user? Is it visual through an indication on the screen? Is it an LED light on your device (sent via operating system control) or do you get an audio notification (also sent via operating system control)? Or is there a combination? The app might allow certain notifications while dismissing others and putting them in the background [in order to avoid being] interrupted.

There are many possibilities, and equivalence partitioning can help you identify them.

You should also consider connectivity, data requirements, and data plans if your app downloads and uploads data, especially if it can do so over a cellular network.

Power consumption is another test design consideration that might be new to you if you cut your teeth testing desktop PC apps. With a desktop PC app, you never have to worry about power consumption. As long as you're plugged into the wall, your app can make the disk spin all it wants; it can do all sorts of really intense graphics on the screen, and it can run the CPU at 100 percent. After all, you have 110 volts or 220 volts (or whatever your main power supply voltage is) reliably coming out of the wall.

That's not the situation at all with those little batteries you have in most mobile devices. With a small battery, you've got a limited amount of time and a limited amount of power. Further, it's different to reliable power coming out of the wall. A battery is a chemical thing, storing and generating power from an ongoing series of chemical reactions. If you use it a lot, it starts to heat up. If you use it a lot, that changes its behavior. So, you must consider power consumption and battery behavior during test design.

As one of the reviewers of this book wrote,

> Using your app and charging your device can also create dramatic heat and [even potentially] burn out the cell modem. However, the app can control the situation, shutting down the app based on a threshold value and starting the app again based on a known safe temperature value. For example, iPhones will display an error message on the screen if the temperature gets too hot, shutting down all apps. But apps can avoid this situation if thresholds are built into the app, with the help of the operating system. Dangerous temperatures are greater than 80C degrees, while a safer temperature range is with a 55C to 60C degrees [threshold]. Again, having this knowledge ahead of time can help to mitigate disasters.

If you test your apps on devices that are plugged into the wall all day, it's not realistic; it's not only unrealistic in terms of power but also in terms of device location. Real devices get moved around. This means the device—and thus your app—must deal with signal strength variations. Changing location can also affect the device's temperature, which can affect your app. For example, if your app is used outside a lot, the device could get hot, which affects device performance and might even result in the device shutting down. This will be exacerbated if your app consumes a lot of power, because that has the effect of making the device hot too.

Technical details about the operating system and your application's architecture will also influence how you design your tests. For example, I have mentioned issues I had with a smartphone and its unreliable OS that required frequent reboots (p. 64). That, combined with the podcast app's inability to keep track of episodes on the SD card made the app almost unusable. I doubt anyone ever tested that scenario.

Information gathering

Now, where do you find out all this information? Well, you know it would be nice to get complete specifications, but that's unusual outside the realm of safety-critical and regulated applications. So, you should look at the specs, certainly, but also pursue other sources of information. We discussed risk analysis in the previous chapter, which is one source. You should talk to people both inside the project and elsewhere in the organization. Experiment with the supported devices, with your app, and with other apps on the devices to learn more about device and app functionality. Another way to learn more about the devices is to read the technical specs online, read online reviews of the devices, and other credible sources of information from third parties.

Regarding gathering information, one reviewer of this book had a number of valuable suggestions.

> Testers need to work closely with the app's developers and ask questions regarding inter-dependencies with the system integration. It also really helps if testers can read code and understand what their app is doing when it's doing it. [In addition], reading log files helps to understand what the app is actually doing. Testers [should] watch the app and review the log files and do a comparison.

In your research, pay particular attention to aspects of the supported devices that affect your app or are used by your app. This includes features such as screen size, screen resolution, GPS, magnetometer, the telephony subsystem, gyroscopes, accelerometers and any other sensors that supported devices may include. Gather as much information about device capability as you can for the different supported devices.

Don't assume that device functionality that is the same will work the in the same way on two different devices. For example, if your app uses GPS, the GPS functionality might well work differently on Android phones versus Apple phones.

As I mentioned before, installs, reinstalls, upgrades, and uninstalls are often insufficiently tested, so pay careful attention to those when designing your tests. Test those features thoroughly, because problems with such features have a significant impact on a large number of users. Testing the robustness of these installation processes is even more critical than with standard PC applications because of the likelihood of various kinds of interruptions, notifications, connection state changes, and background or even foreground activities during the process.

In addition, consider the intersection of payment-related behaviors with these install-state processes, including changes from sponsored mode to paid mode or vice versa (if allowed). This is particularly risky if the expiration or cancellation of a subscription payment model needs to trigger an install-state change.

Finally, let me mention non-functional testing. Install-state testing is sometimes considered functional, sometimes non-functional. We are going to discuss non-functional testing a bit later in this chapter, but your tests can blend functional and non-functional elements. For example, testing functional behavior of the app while the server-side component is under heavy load is a smart thing to do, because connection timeouts and data update delays can affect functional behavior.

Applying test techniques to test design

During test design, remember to use the foundational test techniques, and possibly even advanced test techniques. For the moment, we can focus on the foundation techniques:

- **Equivalence partitioning** is one important technique, useful in almost all testing circumstances and a building block of other techniques such as decision tables and pairwise testing. An example of the use of equivalence partitioning is the identification of different supported devices.

- **Boundary value analysis** is an extension of equivalence partitioning where we identify minimum and maximum members of ordered equivalence partitions. An ordered equivalence partitioning is one where, when two members of the partition are not the same, one member is greater than the other member. Boundary values can affect both functional and non-functional behavior, such as testing the minimum and maximum number of players in an online poker game.

- **Decision tables** are useful when testing combinations of conditions that affect actions the application both should and shouldn't take, especially with transactions that occur quickly. For example, if you're paying for an application, there might be different ways to pay for it, such as with credit cards, debit cards, Paypal, and the like. These conditions, and relevant conditions such as zip code and PIN information, might interact to determine how payment behavior works.

- **State-based testing** is useful when the behavior of the system depends on what has happened in the past, and when relevant conditions are subject to change during a process. For example, application behavior will often change based on the type, speed, and state of the connection, and changes to the connection can change the way the system behaves during a process.

- **Use cases** are useful ways to describe normal, exceptional, and error-handling scenarios. For example, consider a video service. We can do things such as view our video queue, add to the queue, remove from the queue, re-order the queue, and so forth.

- **Exploratory testing** is a good way to apply creativity and flexibility to testing tasks. It's especially useful when sequences of events and combinations of conditions are hard to predict or subject to many variations. For example, you can use exploratory testing to look at things like external interruptions that can happen whilst using the app, and whether the app handles those in a sensible fashion.

- The concept of **error guessing**, originally described by Glenford Myers, was later elaborated into the concept of **software attacks** by James Whittaker.[8] An example of an attack would be to try to intercept Wi-Fi information from a router, based on a hypothesis that the router's security might be weak.

- **Defect-based testing** is similar to error guessing, but it's based on defects that have existed in the past rather than on defects you suspect might exist. For example, if you keep a list of defects that you've seen in your app or similar apps, or that you've heard about or read about in similar apps, you can design tests that would expose such defects.

- Finally, consider **combinatorial techniques,** such as **pairwise testing** and **classification trees**, when looking at conditions, configuration options, and the like which are supposed to be independent but which might interact in unexpected and perhaps undesirable ways. For example, if the risk is high enough, you might decide to use pairwise testing to look for interactions between connection types, connectivity settings, and communication features.

---

[8] Myers 1979 book, probably the first on software testing, is *The Art of Software Testing* (third edition 2011, Hoboken, NJ: John Wiley & Sons). Whittaker described software attacks in his series of books on *How to Break Software* (first title released in 2002 by Pearson).

To illustrate the application of one of these techniques to mobile testing, I decided to pick state-based testing. State-based testing is particularly important for mobile apps, because the connection state changes frequently with mobile devices and connectivity affects the behavior of many mobile apps. Consider the following example of connection-state-dependent behavior.

Figure 3.2 Adler app home screen

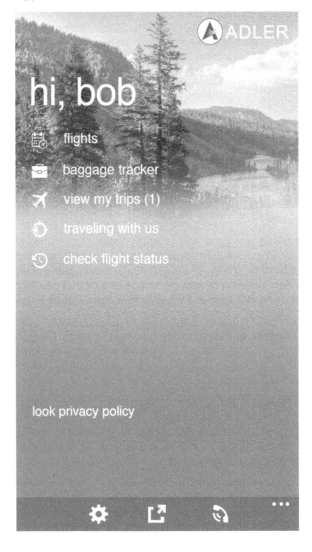

Figure 3.2 shows the Adler app home screen and Figure 3.3 shows the Paloma home screen. Both apps will run whether you've got a connection or not, though certain features don't work without a connection. The type of connection is an issue too.

Figure 3.3 Paloma app home screen

For example, I do a lot of international travel, and one of the things I hate is to get hit with a roaming charge on my bill. So, while I've got almost unlimited data here in the United States, if I'm overseas, my provider will charge me outlandish amounts of money for even the smallest amount of data use. So, when I'm outside the US, I always make sure I have my phone set so that it won't use cellular data.

This means that my apps—at least those that use data—must be able to detect that, while I have a phone connection, I don't have a connection to the internet that will allow me to upload and download data. Both the Adler and the Paloma apps handle this fine on both Android and Kindle devices.

Interestingly, the Netflix app, even though it does store data locally, will not run without a data connection. This is strange because it stores the queue locally. I don't understand why I can't look at the queue without a connection; you can't start the Netflix app at all.

Test design: beyond the classic techniques

Let's look at some additional test design techniques that might be useful for you.

User perspectives and **scenarios** are similar to use cases, but they involve additional details, such as user skill, user location, lighting, weather, connectivity type and strength, accessories and peripherals and device motion. For example, if using an airline travel app to try to fix an itinerary screwed up by an airline mistake—as I was, literally, right before I wrote this paragraph—details could include what type of connectivity you have, how strong the signal is, and whether the signal strength or even connection is varying. Accessories such as a Bluetooth keyboard and headset might be attached. The skill levels of the traveler trying to accomplish the task can be specified as well.

When you get into user skills, you can take that to another level, if you will, and use what is called user **persona testing**. User personas involve trying to put yourself inside the mind of your users. Since mobile app user bases can be very large and diverse, being able to see your app the way your different users do can be very important. Remember, each user is unique in certain ways, but persona testing involves focusing on the way users interact with your app, which you can partition to identify relevant styles of app and mobile device interaction, ways of approaching the app, emotional states and intentions when using the app, and so forth.

For example, consider how a first-time user who knows nothing about your app would use it. Consider how a casual user, somebody who uses your app occasionally, every now and then, would use it. How does the frequent user use your app? The expert? A person who is confused by your app or by mobile device usage in general, which is similar to, but a bit different from, the intimidated user? How about a user who is angry, or similarly impatient? How about a malicious user who is trying to penetrate your app and ultimately your servers? How about someone who is evaluating your app for purposes of a review or to consider using it? How about a user with strong technical skills? How about young users? Old users?

Again, if you are creating an app where you expect—or already have—a very diverse user base, persona testing can be useful for you. It will be easier to determine the relevant user personas—along with the favored and disfavored users—if you have good usability requirements, but that's a rare luxury. We'll return to this topic later.

Finally, developing and using **checklists of important test conditions** for your app is a proven best practice that can help you avoid forgetting anything important in the hurly-burly of each release. The checklists should include major features, the effect of different connection types and speeds, and any different settings or configuration options. You can create these checklists initially using techniques such as equivalence partitioning and boundary value analysis. Over time, as your app evolves, the checklists should evolve with it.

One reviewer of the book commented on the evolution of apps and the challenges of identifying boundary values, writing,

> A problem with mobile testing is that boundaries and thresholds change and oftentimes are not known [in advance]. If the boundaries are not known, [testers need] to work closely with product owners and find out what might be acceptable boundaries. However, limitations are often unknown... [and] threshold values [change], so test accordingly.

Let's look at an example of how user personas affect testing, by using the fictional TallyHo app. I like this app, for the most part, but it does have some occasional weirdness about it. This example is the app on a Windows tablet.

Figure 3.4 TallyHo trip creation

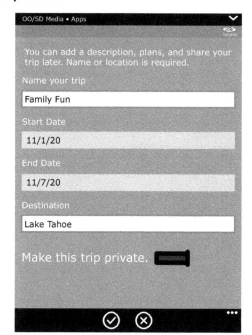

Here's what's weird. If I want to create a trip, I can start doing so, even if I'm offline, as shown in Figure 3.4. However, if I try to save the trip, I get the message shown in Figure 3.5, "Error, cannot create object!" Now, as a technical user, I know enough about programming to have a good idea of what that means, but most users will probably think, "Huh? Cannot create object? What could that mean? I wasn't creating an object, I was creating a trip, which is a concept or a plan, but not an object."

Figure 3.5 Creating a trip fails offline

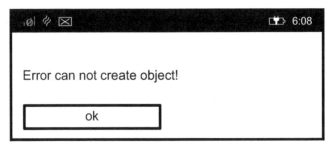

Suppose I create a trip while I'm online. Now it allows me to I save it. However, instead of saying, "Your trip has been saved," it says, "Itinerary updates will appear in a few seconds," as shown in Figure 3.6.

Figure 3.6 TallyHo can save a new trip online, but the message is weird

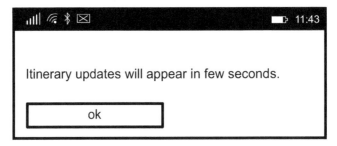

Further, in both cases, the only option is to click "OK", which is confusing. What is it asking me to do? Wait for a few seconds to see what happens? You can imagine that certain kinds of users, such as an angry user, first-time user, intimidated user, or impatient user would be frustrated with either of those situations.

Somebody with a lot of technical experience such as me, can figure out what's going on, though it's not very good. So, when you're thinking about user experience and usability, helpful error messages are definitely part of that equation. Don't put on your literal, computer-programming perspective—assuming you have that background—and say, "Well, those messages are literally accurate, so the software works." The right message not only means literally correct in some programmer-speak interpretation, but suitable to the audience: the various user personas who will see the message.

TestStorming

Let's wind down this discussion of test design with TestStorming, a variation of brainstorming. It's an 11-step process. As you would expect, it's a collaborative technique for identifying test conditions, designing tests, and improving them.

1. The first step is figuring out how you plan to capture the information gathered during the TestStorming session. This can be in the form of mind maps, whiteboards, flipcharts, or spreadsheets.[9]

2. The second step is determining the scope of the session. This involves setting some time limits and a reasonable set of features to consider. After all, you and your colleagues probably won't be able to do all the test analysis and design in a single session.

3. That feeds into the third step, which is focusing on some subset of the larger testing problem, specifically the quality characteristics you consider most important.

4. The fourth step is to assign a facilitator, a session leader. Ideally, this person has testing experience and facilitation experience, as well as strong knowledge of the intended behavior of the mobile app.

5. This brings us to the fifth step, inviting the different participants. As is typical in brainstorming sessions, you want a cross functional team, like the team of stakeholders involved in the risk analysis process described earlier (p. 38). In this context, that means developers, testers and business stakeholders. Now, ideally what we would like from each person on this team is that they are creative, detail oriented, polite, and knowledgeable. The desired knowledge includes intended application usage, organizational goals and testing, and the context of how the application will be used. That's asking a lot of participants. More realistically, aim for a team where everyone is creative, engaged, willing to participate, and able to offer some useful input.

6. Step six is the session itself. It opens with a review of the risks, the requirements, previously discovered defects, and other relevant background information. With this review complete, you ask each participant to identify their top five test conditions. These may be related to items covered in the review or they may be entirely new ideas. After all, it's brainstorming.

7. Step seven is to refine the list of test conditions. This involves identifying and resolving overlap. It involves combining conditions that are basically re-statements of each other, keeping the condition which is worded best or polishing the wording to combine the best of both. It also involves redirecting useful byproducts such as project risks and requirements defects to the appropriate person. Categorizing the test conditions can help the process, and you can use the list of 21 quality risk categories I described earlier (pp. 38–39) as a framework. In addition, as you refine the list, feel free to add variations of the conditions that you notice.

8. Step eight is to review. This involves going through the test conditions that the participants decided to test and effectively wraps up the brainstorming part of the process for the moment.

9. Step nine is where the testers take that set of test conditions and create test cases. You might not create actual test cases for all the conditions. If you plan to use exploratory testing, you might just wrap test charters around some of the conditions. Either way, for each condition you must determine the relevant test oracles. Remember, the test oracles are the things you consult

[9] Personally, mind maps don't work for me, but some people find them useful. I tend to prefer whiteboards.

to assess whether the test results are correct or incorrect. For each condition you must also determine the appropriate depth of coverage.

10. Step 10 is to run the test and log the results, which proceeds as usual for test execution.

11. Finally, step 11 involves determining if there were certain tests that were particularly useful. If so, you capture those for re-use.

The value of TestStorming is like any other process where you collaborate; the team, collectively, has relevant knowledge and experience that will help you avoid missing anything. Could you get many of the same benefits without the actual brainstorming session if you can get stakeholders to review the test conditions that you create as a tester? Yes, probably so, but brainstorming is more powerful in terms of avoiding gaps and also in terms of building consensus.

As an example of TestStorming, consider this travel app, the Adler app on Android, shown in Figure 3.7.

Figure 3.7 The Adler app main menu

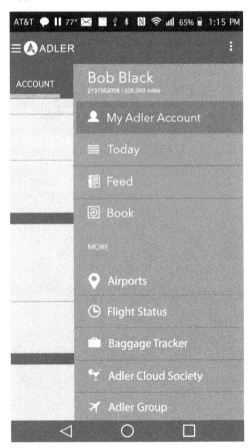

Here are what I would consider my top five test conditions.

1. Certainly, account security ranks in the top five. I don't want somebody using the app to buy tickets for themselves in my name.
2. Also, I want to be able to use the app to quickly get accurate flight status information. If there is a problem with my flight, I want to know about it sooner rather than later.
3. I'm also concerned with the trip management features of various kinds. Do they actually solve my problems? For example, past versions of some airline apps have had a strange usability bug. This bug makes it such that, to find out whether you've got a meal on your flight, you use the window that shows your currently active reservation. You actually have to go out of that window, navigate to the flight-status screen, enter the flight number that you're on, and then scroll down to the amenities icon, and click on text that says "see more". Only at that point will it tell you about whether you have a meal.
4. Streaming video entertainment is another test condition. Fewer and fewer airplanes have entertainment screens on flights now, so the ability to stream movies to the passengers' devices is important.
5. Finally, on the server-side, I definitely want to make sure that my payment information, my passport information and other personal identifying information is stored securely.

Those would be five important test conditions in my opinion. There are others that you might think of as particularly important. In TestStorming, the idea isn't to have each person try to create an exhaustive list of test conditions. Rather, we ask each person to devise their five important test conditions, and collectively across a large enough group you'll get most of the important ones, and you're less likely to miss important test conditions than if you just did it yourself.

3.2 Test your knowledge

Let's try one or more sample exam questions related to the material we've just covered. The answers are found in Appendix C.

Question 2 Learning objective: MOB-3.2.1 (K3) For a given mobile testing project apply the appropriate test design techniques

Consider an application that allows online shopping. It supports the following credit cards: American Express®; Visa; MasterCard®. If you need to test both valid and invalid equivalence partitions, what is the minimum number of tests?

A. three;
B. six;
C. seven;
D. ten.

Question 3 Learning objective: MOB-3.2.2 (K1) Recall the purpose of testing for the correctness of an application

Which TWO of the following attributes are checked during correctness testing?

    A. response time;
    B. suitability;
    C. security;
    D. interoperability;
    E. accuracy.

Question 4 Learning objective: MOB-3.2.3 (K2) Explain the important considerations for planning security testing for a mobile application

A person's credit card information, login ID, and password are captured by a hacker while that person uses free Wi-Fi at a coffee shop to shop online via a mobile website. This is an example of which security planning consideration?

    A. lost devices;
    B. donation of a device;
    C. use of a dodgy app;
    D. ease of attacking mobile devices.

Question 5 Learning objective: MOB-3.2.4 (K2) Summarize the concepts of perspectives and personas for use in mobile application testing

If a person is startled by your application's user interface, they are likely a:

    A. frequent user;
    B. first-time user;
    C. technically knowledgeable user;
    D. impatient user.

Question 6 Learning objective: MOB-3.2.5 (K2) Summarize how device differences may affect testing

If your active-shooter tracking application relies on very precise location information (i.e. within one foot or one-third of a meter) to locate a security threat in a secure area, and this application must run on a wide variety of devices, a primary concern for testing is:

    A. device difference;
    B. security;

C. peripherals;

D. over-the-air upgrade.

Question 7 Learning objective: MOB-3.2.6 (K2) Explain the use of TestStorming for deriving test conditions

TestStorming is:

A. dependent on the requirements;

B. solitary;

C. purely functional;

D. open-ended.

APPLY YOUR KNOWLEDGE

Now, work through an exercise related to the material we've just covered.

The exercise is to create functional tests using appropriate test design techniques. The specific techniques are up to you, but should be appropriate to the behavior you're testing. If you are studying this book with colleagues, you can discuss your solution with them after you create it.

An example solution is found in Appendix B.

3 NON-FUNCTIONAL TESTING

The learning objectives for Chapter 3, Section 3, are as follows:

MOB-3.3.1 (K3) Create a test approach that would achieve stated performance testing goals.

MOB-3.3.2 (K1) Recall aspects of the application that should be tested during performance testing.

MOB-3.3.3 (K2) Explain why real devices are needed when simulators are used for testing.

MOB-3.3.4 (K3) For a given mobile testing project, select the appropriate criteria to be verified with usability testing.

MOB-3.3.5 (K2) Explain the challenges for portability and reliability testing mobile applications.

In this section, we move on to non-functional testing, which is focused on the way in which an app does what it does, rather than what it does, which is its functionality. If you think grammatically, what the app does—its functionality—can be expressed as a verb phrase. For example, a travel app might allow us to create trips, edit trips, share trips with others, and so forth. The way in which the app does what it does—its non-functional behavior—can be thought of as adjectives, adverbs, and other constructs that modify the verb phrases. We want apps to work quickly, reliably, and across supported platforms.

Specifically, we are interested in four areas:

- performance;
- usability;
- portability;
- reliability.

Being a tester, you may have noticed that another typical non-functional character-istic, maintainability, is missing from the list. Maintainability aspects of software are best addressed through static testing techniques such as reviews and static code analysis. These techniques, as discussed in the ISTQB® Certified Tester Foundation syllabus 2018, apply in much the same way for mobile apps as for other types of applications, so we won't have a special section here. I'll refer you to Chapter 3 of the Foundation syllabus.

If you are wondering why security isn't on this list, it has to do with the way the ISTQB® syllabi classified quality characteristics prior to 2018. In the new ISTQB® Foundation 2018 syllabus, security has been moved from being a functional to a non-functional characteristic. Ultimately, who cares whether a particular charac-teristic is categorized as functional or non-functional, as long as you do the tests that need to be done?

Performance testing

Performance testing is about response time, resource utilization, and throughput. Response time is just what it sounds like, which is to say, how long it takes the system to respond to some input or set of inputs. Response time is of greatest interest for interactive aspects of your app.

Resource utilization involves looking at resource consumption under certain levels of load. The particular resources you examine would depend on where you expect bottle-necks to occur. Typically, they include CPU utilization, memory utilization, disk utilization, disk bandwidth utilization, network bandwidth utilization, and so forth.

Throughput is similar to the inverse of response time. For example, throughput for an air-line app would include how many reservations per hour the back-end servers could handle.

Some people would include some additional types of performance testing. Load testing is the ability of a system to handle increasing levels of anticipated, realistic loads. The changes are typically measured in response time, resource utilization, or throughput.

Stress testing is the ability of the system to handle loads at or beyond anticipated or specified limits, with reduced resources, or under other inclement, stressful circumstances. Stress testing involves creating such stressful circumstances, then measuring degradation in terms of response time, resource utilization, throughput, functionality, or data integrity. Stress testing is a good way to identify limits and bottlenecks.

Scalability testing evaluates the ability of the system to grow in terms of users, data, and so forth, without excessive degradation in terms of response time, resource utilization, throughput, functionality, or data integrity. Scalability testing provides metrics that can be used to monitor the production environment to warn of impending limits and to trigger environment enhancement.

In addition to load testing, stress testing, and scalability testing, some people consider additional subtypes of performance testing important. These are beyond the scope of a Foundation-level treatment of mobile app performance testing, but you can find general information about these performance testing subtypes in the ISTQB® Performance Tester syllabus 2018.

Now, for a traditional client–server app or a web-based app, performance testing is complex enough. With mobile apps, you can have all the issues associated with web-based apps, plus performance challenges related to connection type, speed, and reliability. These are major issues on mobile devices, as well as serious resource limitations on the mobile device itself.

Consider the following. Having an app crash because other apps have used up all the memory on a PC is a pretty unusual situation for typical users, unless they keep lots of memory hog apps running as a regular habit. On a mobile device, though, app crashes due to memory exhaustion happen easily and frequently. If you're using something like the hospital and health-care management apps that I mentioned earlier, or even the retail associate handheld app in the home improvement stores that I mentioned, you really need proper performance testing.

Obviously, performance is particularly critical in the health-care situation. If you're trying to figure out someone's blood type for a transfusion, because they have arterial bleeding from a car crash, but instead you're watching the little spinning wheel of misfortune on your app, that's just not good.

Safety is important, but customer satisfaction matters too. Imagine having an associate standing in an aisle staring awkwardly at their iPhone screen and saying, "I'll find you another shovel in just a minute, but first let me watch this little wheel thingy spin around a few more times."

I don't know about you, but if I'm that customer, I will say, "Whatever, you and your wheel thingy have fun spinning around, and in the meantime I'll go to the home improvement store across the street. I'm pretty sure they have shovels."

As another example, I have clients involved with video gaming, including the massive multiplayer video game world. Their servers can have thousands or in some cases millions of players connected to them. In some cases, those people are paying real money to play these games, while in other cases it's just a matter of personal pride, because the games are very competitive. So, these gamers tend to be irritated if performance goes to hell.

Performance testing is a big issue in a lot of different situations, including how the app interacts with the device features like the camera, the voice command activation, Bluetooth, and notifications. When you are performance testing, you have to look at the server-side, assuming there are server-side components, which there usually are. However, fast server-side performance isn't enough. You have to look at the client-side, because there can be a bottleneck on the client app itself.

The bottleneck can also be on the connection. For example, if a system is designed on the assumption that there's always a big, wide data pipeline between the client-side and the server-side, like there usually is with a PC client–server app running in an office or factory, that's not a particularly wise design decision to make for a system that relies on mobile connectivity.

When you're looking at the app itself from the client-side, there are a number of questions to ask about its performance. How long does it take the app to launch if it's not already running? When people are doing other things, are there delays? Is the app sometimes fast, sometimes slow?

If the app is doing something and the users must wait, does it keep the user posted on its status? I personally prefer a progress bar, provided that the progress updates are frequent and accurate. However, as frustrating as the little spinning wheel can be, at least you know that something's happening. If you click on something and the app just sits there, that always makes me wonder, "Hmm, did I click on that icon? Does the app realize that I clicked on the icon?" That often leads me to start clicking over and over again.

You also should consider resource usage, such as CPU, memory, network bandwidth and so forth, as I mentioned. Keep in mind that your app is running on a mobile device and sharing memory and bandwidth and battery power and CPU utilization and all the other resources with a number of other apps. To test this, you need to figure out a typical mix of those other apps, and what they will typically be doing. This aspect of background loads is a critical thing on the client-side, since the resources are so limited.

Another question to consider is how long it takes to get various jobs done—to complete certain use cases—and whether that will be frustrating to people. Performance has an influence on usability.

Don't forget to consider client-side code efficiency, the white-box way of looking at performance. Ideally, you're technical enough to participate in code reviews and look at those kind of issues.

You can't just do performance testing on the client-side. You also need to consider server-side performance. This includes questions such as how long does it takes for a page to get loaded? Are there server delays that can affect your application? Is server resource utilization an issue? What operations are performed on the client-side and what operations involve server interactions is another critical question when designing mobile app performance tests.

These are fairly standard server-side performance testing considerations, which aren't much different from what you'd need to do for a web-based app or client–server app. You need to generate representative incoming load to see whether the server-side performs properly.

Establish performance testing goals

Earlier in the book, I mentioned user personas, and we'll return to this concept with respect to usability later. For the moment, from a performance perspective, you definitely need to consider these different personas and the different use cases that are associated with them.

The implication of user personas for performance is that, when you generate your load on the server-side, it needs to take these personas and their mixes of use cases into account. It also means that you need to consider the personas and their use cases when you are performance testing the client-side.

As the saying goes, "If you don't know where you're going, any road will get you there." It's important to know what your performance goals are before you start running performance tests.

Unfortunately, a lot of organizations don't do this. They just build systems, only to discover that the systems are too slow. Then they try to tune the performance, which doesn't always work. This is a classic testing worst practice, failing to pay attention to key non-functional risks like reliability, performance, and usability until after you've already built the software.

I can hear you thinking, "Yeah, I know that, but where do I get these goals from? When I talk to people, they can't really give me anything concrete. They just say, 'I want it to be fast.'"

Try looking at competing apps. You might very well have some competitors, so download them and benchmark them. You can also benchmark the performance of apps that are not competing but are doing something similar. Benchmark the performance of other apps that your target users use. If you're upgrading an existing app, obviously you don't want it to get any slower. All of these are good sources of performance goals.

Don't leave performance testing to the end of the project or release. Performance test as the system is built. All too often what we see is that organizations wait until right before release to do performance testing, and then the performance results aren't very good. In the worst cases—which are surprisingly frequent—these people discover that tuning isn't enough. They actually have to do major redesigns of the system, which is really expensive and very disruptive to the release schedule.

Getting as close as possible to ideal performance testing

What does the ideal situation look like? Well, ideally, you've got performance tests that kick off automatically as part of your continuous integration framework.

If you can't achieve that ideal, make sure you are careful to run your performance tests frequently enough. We have a client that doesn't run performance tests with every release, they just run them every so often when it occurs to them. That's a risky approach.

When doing performance testing on the client-side, remember to do some (if not most) of the performance testing on the least-resource-supported devices. These are the devices that are most likely to be slow. These kinds of resource-specific performance bugs are not something you can count on a simulator to catch. So, remember to have the cheap, old devices in the test lab; don't just test with the fastest and latest stuff.

In addition, remember that, with native apps especially, there are a lot more client-side considerations than when performance testing a mobile-optimized website. With a mobile-optimized website, most of what will happen from a performance perspective is on the server-side and in the connection, unless there's some real weirdness with what your mobile website is doing on a particular browser.

Even with a mobile-optimized website, remember the stakes in this game. Too slow, like too unreliable or too hard to use, means abandoned.

Let's consider the Adler mobile-optimized website and the native app, shown in Figures 3.8 and 3.9.

Figure 3.8 Adler mobile-optimized website

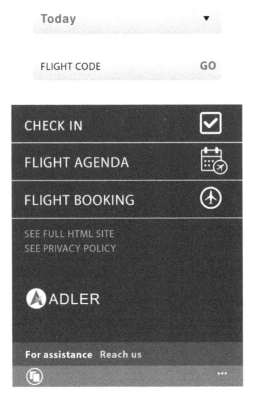

Figure 3.9 Adler native app

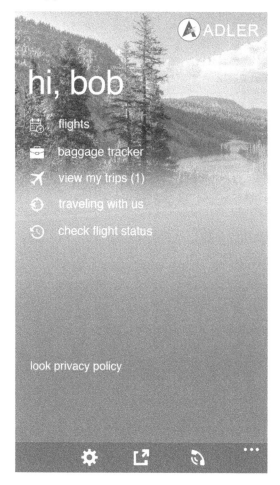

For the mobile-optimized website, most of what I have to worry about in terms of per-formance is on the server-side and the connection. Further, the server-side components are likely the same as those used by the mobile app. So, it's possible to devise some common tests to cover what the native app does and what the mobile-optimized web-site does. For the native app, I also have to worry about the client-side resource utiliza-tion and connectivity, which can be a real issue.

When I do my performance testing for both, I definitely want to do a side-by-side test of the website and the native app. For example, I want to make sure that the time to accomplish a particular task is not too slow on either one, or much slower on one than the other. Due to the nature of the way these two different apps work—web-based versus native—the bottlenecks and performance risks are different. However, remember that the users' expectation is shaped by their overall experience with mobile apps, and the user simply does not care and is not interested in technical reasons why an app is slow.

Also remember to look at other examples of other similar websites. Remember, your users' expectations are heavily influenced by interactions with sites like Amazon and other leading websites. Even though Amazon is not in the travel business, people who use travel apps, like delta.com and the Delta mobile app, have expectations that are formed by these other websites.

APPLY YOUR KNOWLEDGE

Now work through an exercise related to the material we've just covered. An example solution is found in Appendix B.

Here's our exercise, which follows from the previous exercise and continues to use your chosen app. This exercise involves designing a performance testing approach.

First, pick the personas that you think you would need to cover from a performance testing point of view.

Next, determine any client-side and (if appropriate for your app) server-side performance goals.

Decide how frequently you want to do your performance tests, and whether you could integrate your performance tests into a continuous integration framework.

Determine what devices you would use, and why.

Also, consider the use of simulators. I haven't talked about simulators much yet, but in the next chapter we will address the matter thoroughly.

As I said, keep it high level and outline a performance testing approach. Don't try to write a complete performance testing plan.

Usability testing

Let's move on to usability. As I've mentioned already, with mobile app usability you typically have a really diverse and unpredictable user set. That's not true in all cases, such as an enterprise app with a predictable set of users like my home improvement retail client. However, it's typical that there are challenges in anticipating how diverse your user base can be.

You do have to think about all the traditional usability testing issues, such as those addressed in the ISTQB® Advanced Test Analyst syllabus 2012 (colors, sounds, accessibility, and so forth).

For mobile apps, it's also important to think about simplicity. Remember, you're dealing with a relatively small user interface. Your input interface and your output interface are shared from a layout point of view, because, unless you're using an external keyboard, you have the soft keyboard eating a considerable amount of the UI. I've seen situations where the soft keyboard pops up and covers a part of the user interface that you need to be able to see to figure out what the input should be, which is a clear example of somebody not connecting all the usability dots.

The learning curve is important, and, for mobile apps, should be falling-off-a-log easy. You want that forcing function (which I discussed before) to make the app almost self-navigating and entirely natural.

Remember that, if you don't achieve such a level of usability, many times this means that your app gets dumped. Mobile users typically have a very low tolerance for frustrating experiences with difficult-to-use apps.

Utilizing personas

When developing a usability testing approach, personas again are very useful. As mentioned previously, you have various personas, such as the angry user, the impatient user, and so forth.

Some people go beyond the short persona monikers and create a fictional character who fits the persona. For example, I saw one which had Michelle, the traveling executive, who is very tech savvy. Michelle was described in a few paragraphs and a simple drawing, and they also provided a bio. This type of artifact makes it easier to get into character when testing, as you need to act the part.

For example, consider the impatient user. There are different ways to be impatient. However, if I give you two or three paragraphs and a cartoon sketch of a person with steam coming out of his ears, that probably would help you relate to the persona.

As another example, suppose you have to achieve Section 508 accessibility compliance (part of the Rehabilitation Act in the USA) in your application.[10] You would want to have a blind user as one of your personas, along with personas with each of the other disabilities that you have to accommodate, such as sight impaired, hearing impaired, and movement impaired.

When you define your personas, remember that your personas might not just be end users. They could be people who support the system, too. For example, consider the network operations staff for your app's back-end servers. You also have to think about them, because if they make mistakes, then those mistakes impact your customers and users.

Thinking about usability

Considerations for usability testing include the look and feel of the app, color schemes, the overall attractiveness of the user interface and the way it flows, learnability, and understandability.

Consider the example I showed earlier in this chapter, with the travel app when you tried to save trips. There's clearly a real understandability issue there. The messages don't clearly indicate what's going on, so I'm left wondering. What does that mean? How do I interpret that message? Where do I go from here?

---

[10] A good resource to learn more about Section 508 accessibility compliance is www.section508.gov/content/learn/laws-and-policies

Built-in devices and supported peripherals can affect the usability and functionality of your app too. Consider Facebook. Facebook invokes the camera app, so, from the users' point of view, the usability of Facebook now includes the usability of the camera and the camera app. In these situations, you might not be able to do anything about the usability of these devices and peripherals and the apps that support them, but it is something you have to keep in mind. This is yet another reason that mobile app testers must understand as much as possible about their supported platforms, including the hardware, firmware, and operating system capabilities and limitations.

> Usability, like any form of testing, should ideally start before you actually build the app. If you've not tried it, you'll be amazed at what you can get done with HTML or even paper prototypes. For example, as a joint project with the usability designers or the UX team, use index cards to mock-up the different screens and take them to a mall. Identify people who look like your target users, and, in return for some simple gift like a hat or a T-shirt, get them to actually walk through and try to use your app.
>
> This sounds silly, and you might be thinking, "There's no way that will work." It actually does, though. You can get feedback on your proposed user interface before you have spent any time coding anything. We used this approach on a project and got really useful feedback from the dozens of people at the mall.

Once you do get the user interface up, you might be wondering if there's a way to measure or quantify usability. People often say that usability is very squishy and subjective. However, that's not necessarily true.

Suppose we have an app with about 20 use cases associated with it. For example, an airline app would have use cases such as checking status, viewing where the flight currently is, making a reservation, editing a reservation, inputting passport information and so forth. So, when you are running usability tests, keep track of how many tasks you were able to get through in a given period of time. For each of the tasks, track how long it took you, using a stopwatch or timer. Count the number of mistakes made in each task, as the number of mistakes goes up as usability goes down. Count the number of distinct actions necessary to do a task.

Further, when you're repeating tasks multiple times, take those same measurements in each repetition and see how they change, because that tells you something about learnability.

If accessibility is a consideration, whether as a mandatory compliance issue or just something you ought to do, consider measuring usability from the perspective of the different types of disabilities and limitations you are concerned with.

In Figures 3.10 and 3.11 you see the main menus of the Adler app and the Paloma app.

The users of these two apps are pretty much the same, as the target user is the frequent traveler. Looking at these two user interfaces, which do you feel has the better look and

Figure 3.10 Adler app main menu

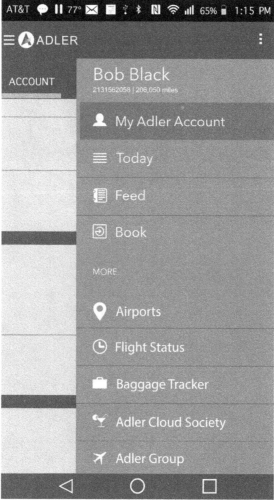

feel or attractiveness? Some training course attendees say they prefer the Adler app, while others prefer the Paloma app.

For these apps, you should identify the 20 or so tasks that you can carry out as part of doing usability testing for them. Identifying the tasks can be done both by inspection of the app and by reflecting on what the users need to do. Another idea is to work with the project team members to rank these tests in terms of product and project priorities to maximize test coverage within project constraints.

In terms of the built-in devices and supported peripherals, for the travel apps these are pretty simple, such as geolocation.

Figure 3.11 Paloma app main menu

If you have a tie-in to an external app, such as United's tie-in to Uber, this can lead to some additional usability tests. Consider the typical use case: I land, fire up the United app, locate my bags, and then call a car with Uber. From the users' perspective, this is all one seamless experience—at least the user wants it to be.

Is an app a competitive advantage? It may be hard for a non-frequent flyer to imagine using anything other than route, convenience, and price to determine the airline you take. However, for a frequent traveler, having a mobile app that most quickly solves the largest number of travel problems is going to be a thumb on the scale.

APPLY YOUR KNOWLEDGE

Now, work through an exercise related to the material we've just covered. An example solution is found in Appendix B.

In this exercise, we continue the previous exercise for the chosen app, but this time outline your usability approach.

First, go back and look at your performance tests. Ask yourself if there are any additional personas to add. Determine your users' expectations with respect to look and feel, attractiveness, learnability and understandability. Identify how your app interacts with built-in devices, supported peripherals, and possibly interoperating apps. Name the different user tasks and use cases associated with them.

Next, you actually do some usability testing, for at least five minutes. First, pick three of the tasks you have identified for your app, and do them in some natural order or just in random order. Keep track of how many tasks you completed and how long it took to perform each task. Track the number of mistakes and the number of distinct actions.

These metrics will allow you to measure how usable your app is and how learnable it is.

Portability testing

Let's move on to portability. You can think of portability testing as addressing the different target environments for the app. Target environments have their own characteristics, so you have to think about the different environments that your app will operate in.

An environment refers not just to devices, but also a whole mix of things that can interact with your app. This includes supported peripherals. It also includes the various types and strengths of signals that you can expect to be available, such as telephony, Wi-Fi, Bluetooth, and so forth. This situation is getting ever more diverse, since there's a race to add more and more capabilities to mobile devices. This means that equivalence partitioning, boundary value analysis, and risk analysis are important, where you test representative items, the most common items, and the most capable and least capable items.

Limits of capability are important from a likelihood-of-failure perspective. For example, if your app handles images, you want to test with the highest and lowest resolution images. It's at the extremes where you often find interesting behaviors. Consider that a high-resolution camera produces larger images, so, if your app depends on using the built-in camera to take a picture and quickly send it to another user, bigger images are not better in this case, they're worse.

Now, you might say, "Shouldn't the developer have already dealt with this?" The developer obviously needs to think about environment differences and how those differences affect behaviors. However, from a test point of view, you have to try to think of the ones the developer might have forgotten about. You should ask the developers about these differences, but remember that what the developer tells you are those differences he or she already considered during development.

For portability testing, one key thing to remember is that the user expects that such differences, when they are visible, at least won't interfere with their ability to accomplish their goals with the app, from playing a game, to planning a trip, to filing an expense report. Consider a travel app. I don't care what the differences are. If I'm on their website, if I'm on their app on my tablet, if I'm on their website on my tablet, if I'm on their website on my phone or if I'm on their native app on my phone, I don't care, I just want to be able to solve the same set of problems. For the most part, I want the apps to work the same way, with consistent usability. This expectation is important to keep in mind.

Approach to portability testing

When defining your portability testing approach, consider what's out there now, in terms of devices, operating systems, peripherals, and more. You should also consider where things are going, because the mobile testing world is rapidly evolving.

Unfortunately, simulators and emulators are usually not very helpful for portability testing. Just as an example, let's look at some of the limitations of the Android SDK emulator based on information on the Android website at the time of writing this book.[11] Now, lest I sound like an ingrate, I should point out that the Android SDK and emulator are free, which makes sense since Google wants you to build Android apps. However, there are limitations to what you can do in the emulator, and thus what you can test with it. For example, you can't place or receive an actual phone call. So, if you need to test telephony, you can't within the emulator. You can't use USB connections, so tests that involve USB connections won't work. Similarly, physically attached headphones, SD card insert and eject and Bluetooth don't work either. You can't determine a network connection state, which could be a real issue for many types of tests, since network connection states and their changes are something you often want to test.

You also can't use the emulator to test battery charge levels or the AC charging state. This makes sense, since the emulator is running on a PC, so either there isn't really a battery or it's a much, much larger battery that affects the PC's behavior in a much simpler way than a portable device's battery does. In fact, any sort of unique physical features or limitations of any specific device can't be tested, since they aren't there on the PC.

Now, the point here is not to argue that emulators are useless for testing. There are many useful ways to employ emulators in mobile app testing, including getting started testing earlier than you could if you only used real devices. However, for portability tests, they're pretty limited.

As I mentioned, your portability testing approach must take into account not just where we are now but also where mobile devices and apps are headed. Stay aware of trends in terms of new capabilities and features that are coming out for the devices, operating systems, and other new apps. Not only do new things come, but existing things go, so

---

[11] See https://developer.android.com/studio/run/emulator

what's important now could become less so in the future. These trends will impact your testing, your app, and people's expectations.

Portability, like some other quality characteristics, must often be balanced against other considerations. For example, if your company wants to improve performance and reliability, that often involves optimizing the app for the hardware. Optimizing the app for the hardware can also make more device features available. However, when you optimize an app for the hardware, portability can suffer.

So, it's smart to have an early cross-functional discussion about the relative importance of portability versus reliability, performance, and capability. If you don't talk about this early, access to hardware-specific features can creep into your app without an understanding of the implications. For example, if you start by just supporting Apple iPhones, the temptation will be to optimize for the iPhone and its capabilities. However, if you do that, one day you'll find, when you try to port the app from the iPhone to Android phones, you can run into real issues. That's especially true because there are many different Android devices.

Another example of this kind of problem can occur when your developers optimize their coding to the most recent hardware, and eventually you have to support previous versions of the platform with less memory, storage, or CPU bandwidth.

Reliability testing

Reliability is a real concern for all kinds of apps. At best, you're going to frustrate users if you deliver an unreliable app. In the worst case, if you're delivering a mission-critical or safety-critical app, reliability issues could result in serious financial or physical damage.

Consider my health-care management client. If a doctor is in the middle of getting information on some sort of procedure using a mobile device and the app crashes, this could be a serious problem if the doctor is performing an operation.

Reliability considerations

What are some considerations for reliability? First off, we want consistency, where the app works the same under the same conditions, every time. It shouldn't go through periods where it's balky, and fails to respond to input, then abruptly comes back to life and starts responding again. Sadly, such behavior is very common.

You also want the app to be robust and fault tolerant. If something goes wrong, the app should respond in an intelligent, hardy fashion. For example, suppose one of the things your app can do is access the camera. Suppose that you try to use that feature to access the camera, but for some reason or another the operating system or the app that controls the camera fails to respond. So, your app has now failed to access the camera. However, that shouldn't cause the app to crash. Ideally, your app responds with a helpful error message, such as, "Cannot access the camera right now, do you want to retry?"

Another aspect of reliability is the ability to get back in working order after something goes wrong. If the app does fail, it should recover quickly. By "recover" I mean that the app returns to a fully operational state. For example, recovery for a mobile device does not just mean that the device reboots fast. Recovery is about how long it takes for all the apps to be up and running again, and able to do what they were doing before the crash.

Now, similar to performance testing, reliability testing has client-side elements and server-side elements. For the server-side elements, the ISTQB® Advanced Technical Test Analyst syllabus 2012 discusses the various kinds of server-side reliability issues that you need to consider, such as frequency of failure, the speed with which it recovers from failure, and the ability to tolerate adverse external events.[12]

For the client-side elements, you need to consider the reliability of the app in response to potentially disruptive events. For example, when your app has a connection via Wi-Fi or Bluetooth, how does your app respond when the connection drops, reconnects, or changes in some other way? Similarly, check what happens with battery and charge state changes, such as letting the battery get really, really low or connecting and disconnecting a charger frequently?

Now, these types of challenging reliability events aren't beyond what a PC app would face, but mobile devices inflict their own reliability challenges on apps. For example, what if the device overheats? What if a hardware sensor or peripheral fails?

For example, if I turn off a Bluetooth keyboard while I'm in the middle of typing something into the app, it shouldn't cause the app to crash, nor should the app hang indefinitely until the keyboard comes back. Instead, the app should seamlessly revert to the soft keyboard, and, if the Bluetooth keyboard reconnects, it should seamlessly shift back to the external keyboard.

The scarceness of shared resources is another source of reliability challenges. You have limited storage, memory, and CPU resources. Further, you can have situations where memory leaks mean that even less memory is available than there should be. Making this even tougher on your app is the fact that you typically have a number of cohabiting applications, some of which are running invisibly in the background. What happens to your app when a memory hog or network bandwidth hog background app consumes large—and perhaps varying—amounts of these resources?

In spite of the odd name, "dumb monkeys" are useful tools for reliability testing.[13] Dumb monkeys are simple tools that can generate large volumes of random input and send that input to your app. Such tools are called dumb monkeys because they have a very simple test oracle, one that is only capable of detecting whether the app has crashed, and, when it does, how long it takes to recover.

Dumb monkeys can be really useful for extended reliability tests, especially to determine mean time between failure and availability. Availability involves measuring not only mean time between failure, but also mean time to repair. Between these two metrics, we can determine how often the app goes down and how long it takes to come back up, which allows us to calculate expected downtime per month or year, which is effectively the inverse of availability.

---

[12] You can find the ISTQB Advanced Technical Test Analyst syllabus on www.istqb.org/downloads/summary/10-advanced-level-syllabus-2012/55-advanced-level-syllabus-2012-technical-test-analyst.html
[13] An article describing dumb monkeys can be found here: https://rbcs-us.com/consulting/jump-starts/test-automation-case-study/

Like performance, portability, and usability, reliability is influenced by the configuration options you support. As I've emphasized throughout this book, if you try to support all mobile devices, you're never going to achieve adequate coverage. There's a rule that applies here, sometimes called the peanut butter rule, which says that, the more you spread it, the thinner it gets.

It's better to pick what your organization thinks will be the most popular devices and operating systems for your particular application and your target users. Then, you can focus your portability, reliability, usability, and performance testing on those devices.

For example, on the Android phone, I can access Adler Studio for streaming entertainment. However, on an unsupported smartphone, if you try to access Adler Studio, it returns a polite and helpful error message, shown in Figure 3.12.

Figure 3.12 Some devices work, and some don't

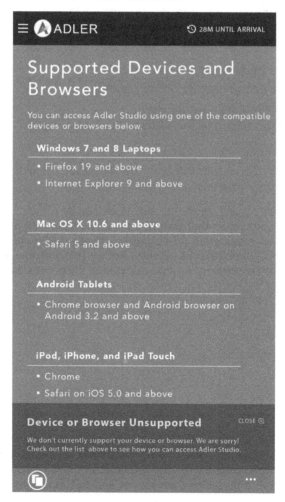

Of course, the error message is only helpful if you have one of the other supported devices, but it's not unrealistic to think that someone with an unsupported smartphone might also have an Android tablet or iPad.

3.3 Test your knowledge

Let's try one or more sample exam questions related to the material we've just covered. The answers are found in Appendix C.

Question 8 Learning objectives: MOB-3.3.1 (K3) Create a test approach that would achieve stated performance testing goals and MOB-3.3.3 (K2) Explain why real devices are needed when simulators are used for testing

You are testing an application that should work on devices with many parallel applications running. The application must gather images and weather readings from devices accessible via the local area network and the internet, and process that data in real time. Which limitation associated with simulators would influence how you used them in performance testing this application?

    A.   differences in CPU and memory utilization;
    B.   problems with generating incoming data;
    C.   unavailability of relevant simulator;
    D.   lack of performance testing skills.

Question 9 Learning objective: MOB-3.3.2 (K1) Recall aspects of the application that should be tested during performance testing

You are testing an application that should work on devices with many parallel applications running. The application must gather images and weather readings from devices accessible via the local area network and the internet, and process those data in real time. Which measurement is most relevant to the processing mentioned here?

    A.   application launch time;
    B.   user interface delays;
    C.   usability assessment;
    D.   irregular performance.

Question 10 Learning objective: MOB-3.3.4 (K3) For a given mobile testing project, select the appropriate criteria to be verified with usability testing

Your active-shooter tracking application uses precise location information to locate security threats in a secure area. This application must run on a wide variety of devices, and be usable by trained personnel and untrained personnel. A primary measurement during usability testing is:

A. number of different tasks completed;
B. time to complete a task;
C. resource usage;
D. simplicity.

Question 11 Learning objective: MOB-3.3.5 (K2) Explain the challenges for portability and reliability testing mobile applications

You are testing an application that should work on devices with many parallel applications running. The application must gather images and weather readings from devices accessible via the local area network and the internet, and process that data in real time. Which reliability measurement is specific to the mobile aspect of this application?

A. resource utilization;
B. mean time between failure;
C. power consumption;
D. loss of connectivity.

In this important chapter, we addressed how test design and implementation differ for mobile apps. We started with functional testing, including security, interoperability, compatibility, accuracy, and suitability. We covered various traditional and untraditional techniques for creating functional mobile tests. Next, we discussed non-functional testing, specifically performance, usability, reliability, and portability.

4 ENVIRONMENTS AND TOOLS

One important way that mobile app testing differs from other kinds of software testing is in terms of environments. Another important difference has to do with the tools used to support mobile app testing. So, in this chapter, we will address tools, including tools for performance testing and functional test automation. We'll also address test environments, how the type of mobile app you're testing affects your test environment needs, and how you can assemble a mix of test environment resources that will address your testing needs while staying within your budgetary constraints.

CHAPTER SECTIONS

Chapter 4, Environments and Tools, contains the following six sections:

1. Tools
2. Environments and protocols
3. Specific application-based environment considerations
4. Real devices, simulators, emulators, and the cloud
5. Performance test tools and support
6. Test automation

CHAPTER TERMS

The terms to remember for Chapter 4 are as follows:

- emulator;
- native device;
- simulator.

1 TOOLS

The learning objectives for Chapter 4, Section 1, are:

MOB-4.1.1   (K1) Recall the expected capabilities for mobile application testing tools.

MOB-4.1.2 (K2) Explain the use of generic tools in testing mobile applications.

MOB-4.x.1 (K3) For a given mobile testing project, select the appropriate tools and environments for testing.

You'll notice this odd-looking learning objective, with the sequence number 4.x.1. You might ask, "What does that x mean?" Well, the sequence number 4.1.1 means Chapter 4, Section 1, first learning objective. The sequence number 4.1.2 means Chapter 4, Section 1, second learning objective. So, 4.x.1 means Chapter 4, general learning objective covering multiple sections in Chapter 4, the first general learning objective for this chapter. In other words, in this chapter on environments and tools, this learning objective spans multiple sections.

The number of mobile apps is around six million, and keeps growing.[1] There are many different devices and many different tools. In addition, the mobile testing tool market is evolving. So, be careful about making significant test tool decisions and investments. Since things are changing rapidly, you could easily bet on the wrong horse, as the cliché goes.

In the ISTQB® Certified Tester Foundation syllabus 2018 and in the Advanced syllabi, and in my books and classes on those syllabi, you can find detailed information about tools and tool selection. That information is still very relevant—indeed critical—so we'll augment that information here, not replace it.[2]

We can break down the tools you might need into various groups. There are mobile-specific tools, which are certainly evolving rapidly. In addition, there are generic tools such as bug-tracking tools, which are more mature. You have to evaluate these tools differently.

Regardless of the maturity of the tools, your first consideration is your tool require-ments. What do you need to do with the tool? I'd recommend not even looking at tools on the internet until you've spent time answering these questions:

- In terms of environments and protocols, do you need the tool to address those?

- Are there multiple environments or protocols you need to test?

- Do you need to simulate different devices?

- Do you need to simulate users, or multiple simultaneous users, for performance testing?

- Can the tool help you with the remarkable and expanding diversity of mobile operating systems and versions?

---

[1] One source of statistics on mobile apps is found at the link here, among many other internet sources of such facts and figures: https://www.statista.com/topics/1002/mobile-app-usage/

[2] The ISTQB® Foundation and Advanced syllabi 2018 can be found at www.istqb.org. My books on the ISTQB® program include *Foundations of Software Testing* (third edition, 2012, Boston, MA: Cengage Learning EMEA) with Dorothy Graham and Erik van Veenendaal, *Agile Testing Foundations* (2017, Swindon: BCS), *Advanced Software Testing: Volume 1* (2e, 2015, San Rafael, CA: Rocky Nook), *Advanced Software Testing: Volume 2* (second edition, 2014, San Rafael, CA: Rocky Nook), *Advanced Software Testing: Volume 3* (second edition, 2015, San Rafael, CA: Rocky Nook) with Jamie Mitchell, and *The Expert Test Manager* (2015, San Rafael, CA: Rocky Nook).

- Do you need to do location simulation?

- Do you need to test various network speeds, network types, quality of service, network connectivity state changes, and other reliability issues?

- Do you need the tool to have the ability to work with simulators, or is it okay if it only works on real devices?

- Do you need the tool to handle input and output issues such as captchas and optical character recognition on text?

Remember not to be dazzled by what's cool about the tool. Way too many bad tool debacles start with some variation of two or three key stakeholders being mesmerized by a well-crafted—but ultimately irrelevant—tool demo created by a tool vendor or open-source tool fanboy.

Don't chase the bright shiny object. Focus. What do you need the tool to do in order to test your app? What are the different test environments you need the tool to work in? What kind of tests do you need to run?

There are critical tool-related skills issues, too. How hard is it going to be to use the tool? Do you have people who can't use the tool, due to skills or accessibility issues?

Can you trust the vendor or open-source community behind the tool? Part of this is simply about longevity, as the best tool in the world gets really useless really quickly after the vendor who makes it goes out of business. It's also about long-term direction and the level of commitment the vendor has to your particular niche and needs. Can you trust the vendor or community to continue to evolve the tool, to keep it up to date and relevant to your needs?

That's not a complete list, but it should get you started thinking about things you need to look for in a tool.

Suppose you get the wrong answers to some of these questions? Again, there's no long-term benefit to rushing a tool decision. There's no prize for a stupid decision made very quickly. Go slow. Remember that the mobile tool market is still immature. There will be a lot of casualties, a lot of vendors and tools dropping out. In addition, if you're new to mobile app testing, or even testing itself, you've probably got a lot to figure out as well. Because of the constant evolution of the tools, keep in mind that if there is an issue and you can't find a good tool now, that problem might resolve itself after six months or a year.

Some people say, "Well, look, with all the free tools out there, there's no harm in trying stuff, right?" Remember this: free test tools are like free puppies, only not as cute and they won't lick your face. If you've never heard this joke, the point is—at the risk of making the joke entirely unfunny by explaining it—that a free puppy is free to get but not free to have. Puppies eat, puppies get sick and need to go to the vet, puppies need shots, puppies poop in the house, and puppies chew things up. Sometimes puppies die and make everyone really, really sad. Well, free tools can cost a lot, do a lot of damage, create stinky situations, and make people really sad, too.

Generic testing tools

In mobile testing, you will often have a need for generic tools, the kind you'd use in testing pretty much anything. You'll need tools for test management, either a classic test management tool or an Agile task management tool adapted to the purpose. You'll need to manage defects. If you're in an Agile world, you probably have user story management in your task management tool, but, if not, you'll need some sort of requirements management tool.

All software projects need build and configuration management tools. Further, whether you're Agile or not, you should try to exploit the potential of continuous integration tools, static analysis tools, and unit testing.

You should also consider server-side testing tools, which would be the fairly typical tools used for web-based application testing, web services testing, and so forth. After all, for the server-side components, whether the incoming traffic comes from a mobile-optimized website, a hybrid app, or a native app, it doesn't really matter to the server. It just looks like incoming traffic in the form of HTTP, FTP, HTTPS, some other standard protocol or some custom interface. So, the usual tools necessary for testing server-side components apply.

Figure 4.1 Adler app and Adler mobile-optimized website, side by side

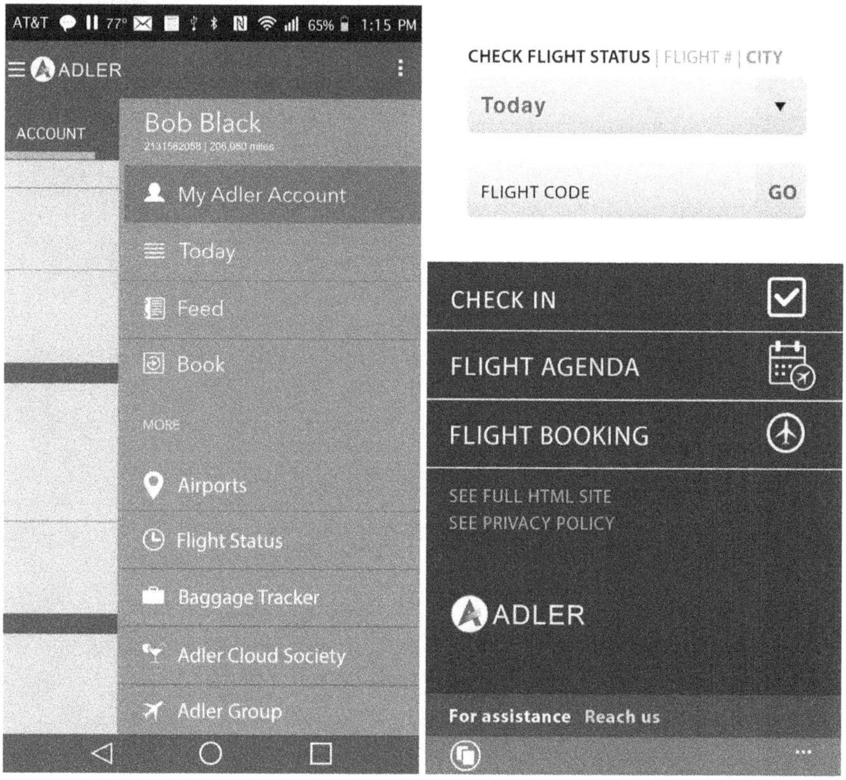

Here we see the Adler app and the Adler mobile-optimized website. Both rely on server-side services, so there are functionality, reliability, performance, and security characteristics to be tested on the server-side. When you test functionality, reliability, performance, and security, you should consider testing directly on the servers and also through the apps to the servers, because it often makes sense to do both.

One way to approach adding features to your mobile apps is to add the capability to the server but don't make it accessible to anybody via your apps at first. You put the feature support components on the server, but not on the client, and you test them on the server. After those work, you can enable them on the mobile-optimized website, which is usually easiest. Ultimately, you enable the features on the native app itself.

One potential issue with that approach is siloing. This happens when you have separate teams in charge of the server-side, the mobile-optimized website, and the native mobile apps, with perhaps a separate team for each native mobile app operating system. Such an organizational approach can create issues, not only, but especially, in terms of your testing. This is a bigger issue, but you need to make sure that there's coordination across these teams, and that there's not some fantasy that system integration and portability problems can be easily surfaced and solved in the course of your testing.

Commercial vs open-source tools

Something I find interesting about tools is how much some people have their minds made up on this whole issue of commercial versus open source, and come down firmly on one side or the other. That kind of Manichaean thinking closes a lot of doors.

If you have decided commercial tools are the only way to go, well, I can tell you that I have a lot of clients that are very successfully using open-source software either directly, or taking those tools and modifying them to do what they need the tools to do. So, certainly, consider open source.

However, if you're an open-source devotee, don't totally dismiss the commercial tools. There can be some advantages there, too.

One of the biggest mistakes that people make with tools is that they fail to sit down and carefully analyze their goals, requirements, and constraints prior to making a tool decision. Open-source devotees just focus on cost. "Open source is free," they say, "so we're going to do that," forgetting my earlier metaphor about free puppies not actually being free.

Believers in commercial tools many times say, "Look, we gotta have support, so we gotta go commercial," forgetting examples such as Red Hat Linux where you actually can buy commercial support.

So, carefully analyze and document your requirements. (Yes, Agile folks, I said to document them, because you're likely to have dozens—if not a hundred—functional and non-functional requirements, which is way too many to remember.)

Making a decision

When you analyze your requirements, address the questions I raised earlier, and more, such as the following:

- What do you actually need the tool to do?
- Do you need commercial, external, or other professional support?
- How will you address tool maintenance, especially considering that the mobile world is rapidly changing?
- What kinds of tests do you need to automate and how will the tool actually execute those tests?
- Is there a reliable test oracle?
- How will you run tests over a long sequence of releases with very low false positive and false negative rates?
- Is it possible that the tool will create a lot of so-called "flaky tests" that sometimes return false positives and other times pass?
- Is it possible that the tool will create a lot of unmaintainable tests that produce a lot of false positives any time the slightest thing changes?
- What is the business case for automation? In this business case, have you clearly addressed issues of short-term and long-term costs, efficiency, effectiveness, speed, and accuracy benefits, risks, and opportunities?
- Have you considered both short-term and long-term issues?

As I said, proceed carefully in this analysis and document your goals, requirements, and constraints. As a rule of thumb, for any tool that plays a significant role in your testing, if you haven't come up with at least a few dozen requirements, you haven't thought about it enough. Further, if you've only asked yourself these questions, you haven't talked to nearly enough people.

As an example, I did this exercise for a client recently. They are in the health-care facility management business. For their test management tool, I came up with over 100 functional and non-functional requirements. I interviewed about 30 people in the organization, both participants in the testing process and stakeholders in the system under test.

Once you've come up with the requirements, then and only then is it time to start looking at the tools. Using the requirements and constraints, you can create a short list of tools that you want to consider. Now is the time to carry out pilot projects and evaluate the results of each pilot against your business case.

Throughout this process, remember the aphorism: marry in haste; repent at leisure.

To illustrate the incredible variety of tools available, suppose you were building an app that uses Bluetooth to communicate with various sensors. If you were building an app like that, you might need to be able to test functionality and security with the different peripherals you will support. You probably also want to look at performance and reliability, too, by simulating streams of incoming traffic.

Believe it or not, not only is there a tool out there for that, there are actually a couple. Further, remember that, if you can't find the right tool, you can build your own. There are professional technical testers, often called toolsmiths, with strong competencies in building custom tools. However, that should be the last resort, not the first. It's almost always more expensive to build your own tool than to use a commercial tool or to use open source.

4.1 Test your knowledge

Let's try one or more sample exam questions related to the material we've just covered. The answers are found in Appendix C.

Question 1 Learning objective: MOB-4.1.1 (K1) Recall the expected capabilities for mobile application testing tools

Which of the following is a mobile-specific test tool capability?

    A. browser independence;
    B. simulating changing location;
    C. working with various network speeds;
    D. simulating loss of network connectivity.

Question 2 Learning objective: MOB-4.1.2 (K2) Explain the use of generic tools in testing mobile applications

Which of the following tools is the best example of a generic tool that is useful in any mobile testing project?

    A. web server performance test tool;
    B. Android platform simulator;
    C. telecom mobile protocol simulator;
    D. bug-tracking tool.

APPLY YOUR KNOWLEDGE

Now, work through an exercise related to the material we've just covered. An example solution is found in Appendix B.

First, for your chosen app, determine what types of tests you need to automate on the device itself and/or on the server. You should consider functional testing, especially regression testing, which is usually a big issue, especially in Agile life cycles. You should also consider performance and reliability, which could be a big issue if your application does something critical. Also consider security if you think it is a concern. Finally, consider portability if your app runs on multiple, different devices.

Now, search the web to find at least one commercial option and one open-source option. You're almost certain to be able to find such tools out there.

If you are working as part of a group, you can discuss your results with your colleagues.

2 ENVIRONMENTS AND PROTOCOLS

The learning objectives for Chapter 4, Section 2, are:

MOB-4.2.1   (K1) Recall the sources of data for a mobile application.

MOB-4.x.1   (K3) For a given mobile testing project, select the appropriate tools and environments for testing.

Earlier in this book, I gave the example of my client that gave iPhones to all the sales associates in their stores (p. 9). Because of that, they have a fairly homogeneous environment. This is true not only of the client-side, but also the connectivity in the stores (through the in-store Wi-Fi installed by them) and the back-end servers in the stores and in their data centers.

In terms of mobile testing, this homogeneity makes them the exception that proves the rule, as the saying goes. They don't have to deal with widespread and unpredictable environmental diversity. What diversity they do have is due to deliberate decisions. For example, they have to depreciate the iPhones, so over time there came to be multiple generations of iPhones in stores.

Alternatively, consider an organization that's building an app for Android devices. There are a lot of different Android phones out there. Further, as we discussed earlier, the Android phone vendors continue to add new features, which helps them avoid the commoditization fate that befell the makers of PCs. This constant stream of new features and updates means yet more diversity because you've got to support the previous stuff as well as the new stuff and the changed stuff.

So, in general, the level of variation with mobile environments is much higher than PCs or laptops. People entering mobile testing sometimes make the mistake of thinking, "Okay, it's a smaller screen and a soft keyboard—except when we use a Bluetooth keyboard—so how different could it be from testing PC apps?" Well, the differences can be very significant and very important for testing.

Now, the gold standard of software testing is an environment that is an identical replica of the production environment. That's always a challenge, even with homogeneous environments. However, in mobile testing, given the diversity of environments, production replica test environments are often impossible, not only due to cost, but also due to the inability to know for sure what your user base is doing.

So, in this section, we look at some things you need to think about in terms of your test environments.

Connectivity and memory

Most mobile apps rely to some extent—often a great extent—on data connectivity to enable their functionality. So, data connectivity is a key element in your test environments. This includes, obviously, both cellular and Wi-Fi connectivity. However, if you're thinking, "That's easy enough, because cellular connectivity is cellular, and Wi-Fi connectivity is Wi-Fi," well, no, it's not that simple.

For one thing, cellular networks continue to advance in terms of their technologies, and mobile devices usually support current and previous technologies. So, my connection changes as I move around, towards or away from the cell tower, both in type of connection and strength of signal, and perhaps my connection gets handed off to another cell tower during a data transfer.

There are similar issues with Wi-Fi. You have different standards and frequencies and thus speeds. Signal strength and connection type can vary as you move in relation to the access point you're connected to, and you can get handed off to another access point during a data transfer here, too. To experience this—or to test it on your app—go to a public place like a mall, airport, or hotel and walk around while doing intensive data transfers such as emailing image attachments and downloading or streaming audio or video.

You also have non-network connectivity that can affect your app or be used by your app, such as near-field communication (NFC), Bluetooth, USB, HDMI, infrared, and more. You can have proprietary types of connectivity, such as the LG phone that has an ability to do screen mirroring on LG TVs.

Again, the nature of mobile apps is to be used in a mobile and dynamic setting, so not only do you have to consider all these modes of connectivity, you also have to think about what happens with them. For example, how reliable are they? In situations where people might be moving around, what happens if the connection is lost and then reestablished? What happens if the throughput rates go up and down because people are moving and because network usage by others varies? How do such changes in throughput and connectivity interact with over-the-air app installations, updates, uploads, or downloads?

For example, the built-in podcast app on one of my older smartphones exhibited a particularly irritating bug in this regard. To be able to listen to podcasts offline, it had to be able to download and store the episodes, not just stream them. It can take a while to download a podcast if it's an hour long news podcast, especially if it's a video podcast. Now, that's unavoidable, but here's the bug: if the app was part way through the download—no matter if at 10 percent, 50 percent, 75 percent or even 99 percent—and the connection dropped, the app would give a failure message, delete however much of the file it had downloaded, and then immediately start over. Worse yet, if you had four or five episodes queued up to be downloaded, it would start on the same file it had failed on, which could result in an almost endless loop of failures if that particular podcast file was big. And oh yeah, the same brain-dead behavior occurred when the connection dropped or timed out on the podcast host server-side, such as when the server's local network was congested or the server itself was overloaded. The whole thing was really frustrating.

This is the type of thing you need to test. Signals will go up and down, vary in strength, and change in type. If your app downloads or uploads data, it should keep track of how much has been received or sent, so it can simply resume when interruptions occur. Don't make your users watch the app retry over and over again, or, worse yet, force the user to initiate the retries. Use equivalence partitioning to identify different events that can result in interruption, as well as boundary value analysis to identify minimum acceptable download speeds, and make sure you cover those.

Another important consideration is memory and storage, which is similar in complexity to connectivity. You have the random access memory (RAM) which is used by all running programs. There are also various kinds of file storage, such as the built-in storage, SD cards and potentially external storage, such as a USB flash drive connected to an Android phone. For the different types of file storage, you need to use equivalence partitioning and also boundary value analysis, because minimums and maximums are important for storage and memory.

Like connectivity, memory and storage are shared resources. So, you must not only look at your app's use of memory and storage space, you also have to look at your app's interaction with other apps via memory and storage, and how cohabiting apps can affect your app. For example, some apps running on a mobile device can be memory hogs and storage hogs, not just CPU hogs and network throughput hogs.

A problem specific to memory is the potential for memory leaks. A memory leak can happen when data is allocated from what's called heap storage. This is a little technical, but I hope I can explain it even if your background isn't programming, because it's useful to understand how this works.

In typical programming languages, there are two types of memory a program can use while it's running, heap and stack. You can think of stack memory as similar to a deck of cards, with cards representing chunks of information that the program wants to use. The deck of cards metaphor isn't perfect, because these cards of information are always added to and removed from the top of the deck only, and the information on each card is available and visible wherever the card is in the deck. The stack is managed in a predefined fashion, according to the rules of the programming language, so this type of memory can't leak, though it can be exhausted.

Now, the heap is a different story. Imagine information being stored in waterproof boxes of various sizes, and thrown into a pool. A box can be retrieved by means of a cord attached to the box any time you want to examine the information in the box or remove the box from the pool. There is a limit to how much total volume of boxes can be put into the pool, because assume you're not allowed to add a box to the pool if it would make the water in the pool overflow the edges.

Now, suppose that someone cuts one of the cords leading to a box, or loses the cord in the pool. That's what a memory leak is like. The box remains in the pool, consuming some of the available volume, but you can't get to the box. Assume you can't dive in and retrieve the box or scoop it up with a net. That bit of available space in the pool for storage is lost. In computer terms, that loss is described as a leak, though I admit that seems a bit opposite to the metaphor I'm using here.

So, with that metaphorical description in place, let me give the more technical explanation of memory leaks, heap memory, and stack memory. Not all programming languages allow the programmer to directly manipulate heap memory, but some programming languages such as C and C++ do. In other programming languages such as Java, the language manipulates the heap memory for you, similar to the stack. In all programming languages that I'm familiar with, the compiler automatically generates software code that controls the stack. When you create variables, the variables go on the stack, but those go away when a particular function ends.

Heap memory is not like that. Heap memory, once allocated by a program, stays allocated as long as the program continues to run or until the program deallocates the memory. This is how memory leaks, because, if heap memory is allocated and then the program loses track of it and doesn't deallocate it, the memory space remains reserved by the program.

So, what can you do about memory leaks? One important tool is reliability testing, as we discussed in Chapter 3. However, it's also important that teams use static analysis and code reviews, because reliability testing for memory leaks can be a hit-or-miss proposition, and memory leak failures are often irreproducible.

Stuff happens, so test for stuff

As I've said, mobile apps exist in a dynamic, changing environment, which means that stuff will happen. That stuff includes various kinds of disruptive events and interruptions that can affect your app. So, when designing and implementing your test environment and your tests, you need to think about how you simulate those kinds of events as realistically as possible.

As I've mentioned, you need to test situations where connections go up and down and change properties. You also have to simulate bottlenecks, because even if you've got a strong connection, you could have a bottleneck somewhere in the network that results in abysmally slow data flows between your app and the server.

Cables can get disconnected. For example, if you have a USB cable and your app is copying files to or from a connected PC, what happens if the USB connection fails because somebody disconnected the cable?

What happens if there are problems on the server-side that result in your app receiving garbled or incomplete information, or no information at all? Your app needs to be robust and provide good, intelligible error messages when those things happen.

I've already mentioned interruptions of downloads, but there are many other types of interruptions. You can have a situation where your app is running or perhaps updating, and some interruption occurs. An interruption could be an incoming call, an incoming text message, a Facebook notification, a Twitter notification, an Instagram notification, breaking news, or any of the other dozens of ways your mobile device and its apps can be interrupted. You may have heard people say something like "my phone exploded," which usually means massive numbers of interrupts from messaging and social media apps. So, test what your app does when someone's phone explodes.

What happens when the battery gets low or even runs out? How do power saving modes affect your app?

Overheating can happen, which changes the behavior of the device and the apps running on it. How will your app respond? This is an especially important question if your app is designed to be used outside. However, as one reviewer of this book mentioned, charging the phone, calling with the phone, or using other apps or devices on the phone generates heat. Overheating can damage the device in the worst case, so you should test your app's ability to monitor temperature and enforce limits.

What happens when a remote device fails? Will that impact your app?

This is a partial list, to get you thinking. Think of all the different things that could go wrong and check to see what happens to your app. Remember, if you don't look first, the users will eventually be exposed to what happens, and it might not be pretty. If so, the users will write reviews on the app stores that say your app is bad because it doesn't handle the real world very well.

Device capabilities and features

In addition to the other items in the environment, you also have to think about the device itself. For example, if your app uses the camera to read QR codes, you must consider the different cameras, camera resolutions, settings that the cameras could have, and so forth.

You should consider screen size. For example, if you've got an app that is designed to display really detailed images, that's not going to look so good on a small screen.

You also need to consider lighting. This is an area where my Android phone has problems. Often, it tries to dim the screen, I assume to try to conserve battery power, based on the ambient light. That's fine, but, when I'm playing videos on my phone, I've noticed fairly frequently that it gets it wrong and it dims it too much.

Does your application use GPS? If so, you have to consider different locations, network connections, and other kinds of connections. Similarly, if your app uses data from accelerometers, gyroscopes, and magnetometers, you need to think about the different variations there.

If your app uses heart rate sensors, you need to consider how those could work and also how they could fail.

At the very least, you'll need to use equivalence partitioning. This starts with identifying all of the different options that can apply to these different factors, and covering those at least once. If you think that these device features are high risk, or that particular kinds of interactions are high risk, then you might use pairwise combinatorial techniques to look at pairs of combinations.

Now, pairwise testing is for testing capabilities and features that are not supposed to interact, to look for inadvertent interactions. When you have capabilities and features that are supposed to interact, and you need to test for proper interaction, that's when you use things like decision tables and domain analysis.

Decision tables are covered at Foundation level. Domain analysis is covered at the Advanced test analyst level (ISTQB®). Domain analysis is a very powerful technique for certain kinds of situations where one or maybe two factors change the way that factors interact.[3]

Data handling and protocols

Part of setting up your test environments is designing and implementing the test data and test data protocols. The mobile device itself is a source of data; for example, from a user typing something in or doing various kinds of gestures, the device can generate data such as GPS information and so forth. Data can be downloaded from a server. There can be some sort of peripheral connected, such as a Bluetooth keyboard, so you can have data that's flowing from outside the device to the device and from the device to the outside. Since many of these situations involve the flow of data onto and off the device, that potentially adds security issues.

You need to consider the different kinds of data that can be sent, received, stored locally, and stored remotely. Equivalence partitioning of the kinds of data that the app sends, receives, and stores, and the way in which it sends, receives, and stores data, is a smart way to approach this.

Be careful, though, not to restrict yourself to purely functional testing. If you do that, you might think, "Okay, the data is fine under all the different functional test conditions, therefore I don't have any data issues." No, you also need to consider reliability. You should run your reliability tests, and, afterward, look at the data to ensure completeness, correctness, and integrity. The same applies with security testing as well as portability and interoperability testing.

When checking these functional and non-functional tests for unwanted side effects on data, be sure to check both the client-side and the server-side.

Look at the different protocols that are used. Are you testing, for example, all the different cellular network types? You should use equivalence partitioning to ensure that you've covered all the different protocols. If you use simulators, ensure that the simulators are adequately covering those protocols as well.

---

[3] Time precludes getting into the difference between equivalence partitioning and pairwise testing, but I refer you to www.pairwise.org if you're not familiar with that. You can read detailed descriptions of pairwise testing, domain analysis, and decision tables in my book, *Advanced Software Testing: Volume 1* (second edition 2015, San Rafael, CA: Rocky Nook).

What does a cubic meter of devices cost?

I was speaking to a small group of a tech folks, CIOs, IT people, developers, and testers in a special consulting session about mobile testing in Moscow. One of them said, "In order to do our testing well, we need a cubic meter of devices in our test lab." Typical Russian sense of humor, very sardonic, which I personally find very funny. Part of the humor of the comment is the element of truth.

A cubic meter is about 60,000 cubic inches or about 30 cubic feet. It's a big box. You probably don't want to buy a cubic meter of devices, especially since you would also have to maintain them. However, what if that's about what you need, device-wise, to test?

Rather than own all of those devices, why not rent, borrow, or virtualize some of them? Obviously, there are some main ones that you need, your core devices; you'll want those in your test environment.

For less central devices, you have various options. There are open device labs. You can use crowdsourcing. You can use test labs. You can use virtualization.

Now, I had a client tell me at a conference that they had completely given up on simulators and emulators for mobile testing. They were doing 100 percent testing on real devices of one kind or another, including cloud-based devices. When I asked why, he said they were testing games, and had found they couldn't get good feedback on how the game would work in a simulator.

However, another client who overheard the remark told me that they use simulators all the time. His app is a relatively standard business application, limited to basic inputs from the keyboard and displaying data.

Devices change and evolve over time. I have one of the earlier Kindles, which was a gift from my mother, who was an early adopter of the Kindle. This is a nice device for reading a book, but that's pretty much all you can do with it. It does have a nice local dictionary feature which allows you to check a word without a network connection too. It has an early, experimental browser for the Kindle as well as experimental text-to-speech features, but I never used those.

I've since moved to a Kindle Fire. That thing is basically an Android Tablet, albeit with a strange limitation that you can't go to the standard Google App Store, but instead must rely on the Amazon App Store, which has fewer choices. However, it can do a lot of stuff. So if you're testing a Kindle Fire, you're basically testing a tablet. You can't assume that the only use case is reading a book on it.

4.2 Test your knowledge

Let's try one or more sample exam questions related to the material we've just covered. The answers are found in Appendix C.

Question 3 Learning objective: MOB-4.2.1 (K1) Recall the sources of data for a mobile application

Which of the following sources of data is most specific to mobile testing?

    A. a web server;

    B. an accelerometer;

    C. a cloud testing service;

    D. a Bluetooth keyboard.

Question 4 Learning objective: MOB-4.x.1 (K3) For a given mobile testing project, select the appropriate tools and environments for testing

Assume that you must set up an environment for testing a brand-new mobile application. The application will run on Apple and Android phones and tablets. Not only will the app allow users to purchase movie tickets online, including reserving seats and ordering food in advance, it also contains some innovative features that your company wants to keep secret prior to release. The app must communicate with a server-side component which you are also building and testing. Because complex graphics are used during seat selection, speed of connection is important. Because transactions must be atomic—that is, either seats are reserved and paid for or no seat is reserved and no charge is made—reliability and performance matter. You are trying to beat your competitors to market with your new features for this application.

Which of the following statements best describes an aspect of the test environment you will need?

    A. You will do almost all app testing on simulators.

    B. You will rely heavily on crowdsourcing to reduce device costs.

    C. You will rely heavily on used and refurbished devices to reduce device costs.

    D. Your test environment will contain load generators.

APPLY YOUR KNOWLEDGE

Now, work through an exercise related to the material we've just covered. An example solution is found in Appendix B.

This is another in our series of exercises in this chapter, where you'll follow on from the previous exercise. In that exercise, we were looking at tools. In this exercise, for your chosen app, think about your test environment. You need to outline how you will address data handling, data protocols, device capabilities and features, the real-world stuff that affects your app, memory and storage issues, and connectivity.

If you are working with a group, you can discuss your solution with the others.

3 SPECIFIC APPLICATION-BASED ENVIRONMENT CONSIDERATIONS

The learning objectives for Chapter 4, Section 3, are:

MOB-4.3.1   (K2) Explain the differences between browser-based and native device applications.

MOB-4.x.1   (K3) For a given mobile testing project, select the appropriate tools and environments for testing.

As I said earlier, the shortest path to delivering a mobile app is to make a mobile-optimized version of your website. Theoretically, you can then run your app on any phone with any supported browser.

This has its limitations, certainly. For one thing, for sites built using mobile-optimization technology instead of responsive website design, there's often an option to switch to the full mobile site; that is, the non-mobile-optimized version. This full site may offer more features than the mobile-optimized site—which is itself a problem—but it looks worse on the mobile device. That can then be compounded by someone selecting a future default to the full site, then forgetting they had done so.

In addition to those issues with the mobile site, there are also performance issues, as everything involves connectivity and many things involve data round-trips, which means you're having to pull data across the internet. Further, there are functional limitations, as there are certain things you can't do; for example, those that involve the device capabilities.

So, when you test a browser-based mobile app, whether mobile-optimized or built with responsive technologies, be sure to address these issues of usability, performance, functional limitations, and definitely browser portability. Don't rely on testing with a PC browser. You need to test supported browsers on different supported mobile devices.

With a native app, you have additional issues of portability, as I mentioned before, but the app can be more usable, faster, and more reliable. It can also potentially do things in an offline mode when you don't have a connection. I say potentially, for some native apps don't. For example, I mentioned the situation with the Netflix app, which doesn't allow you to do anything even though it presumably has data.

With native apps, you'll probably need to use some simulators, especially for performance testing. However, remember the story I told about the gaming company that stopped using simulators entirely, due to the lack of credibility of the results? (p. 111)

If your target device is limited in the market, expect a rough ride. For example, imagine you have to create and test an app for Blackberries, because your particular target customers use them. (Believe it or not, Blackberry apparently still does have users in certain parts of the world and in certain markets.) So, this is going to pose some interesting tool challenges, at least on the client-side. Will you be able to get simulators and functional test tools? You might be able to get performance, reliability, and load test tools, but probably only for the server-side.

Somewhere in-between native apps and browser-based apps are hybrid apps. These have browser-based elements but also native code that provides access to the device's sensors and other device-specific capabilities. In addition, as one reviewer of the book mentioned, there are application program interfaces (APIs) which provide additional capabilities and give the developers ways to re-use existing code. These properties allow the developers to do things they couldn't with a pure browser-based approach, in terms of using the device features.

Sounds great, huh? Well, from a testing point of view, it's the worst of both worlds effectively, because you can have all the testing challenges of both browser-based and native.

Take a look at Figures 4.2, 4.3, and 4.4.

Figure 4.2 Adler native app on Android device

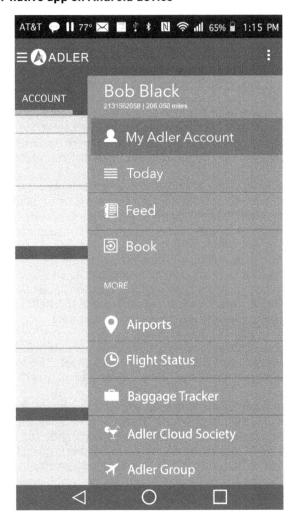

Figure 4.3 Adler app on a Windows device

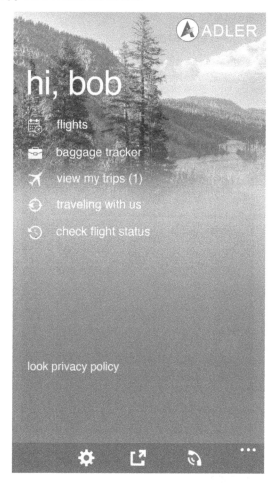

You have the native Adler Android app in Figure 4.2 and the mobile-optimized website in Figure 4.4. As you can see, the user interface is different.

If you compare the native Android app and the native Windows app in Figure 4.3, you can see that the user interface is very different. The Windows app has that interesting forest background. There are actually other backgrounds that display too.

The Android app has a similar layout as the website. It also uses the standard Adler logo.

Since the UI has a similar look and feel to it with both the Android app and the mobile-optimized website, it's a more seamless transition. It's bit more jarring on a Windows tablet if you switch between the native app and the mobile website, because the UI is different.

Figure 4.4 Mobile-optimized Adler website

In terms of the testing, you have to test the supported devices, either yourself or using an outsourced option. The mobile-optimized website is simpler, because you just have to look at browser compatibility testing.

4.3 Test your knowledge

Let's try one or more sample exam questions related to the material we've just covered. The answers are found in Appendix C.

Question 5 Learning objective: MOB-4.3.1 (K2) Explain the differences between browser-based and native device applications

Which of the following is an example of a mobile application bug more likely to be seen with a browser-based application than with a native application?

A.   plug-in incompatibility;

B.   a bug not seen on a simulator;

C.   server-side performance degradation;

D.   lack of tool support.

Question 6 Learning objective: term understanding (K1)

What is an emulator?

A.   A device, computer program, or system that accepts the same inputs and produces the same outputs as a given system.

B.   A device, computer program or system used during testing, which behaves or operates like a given system when provided with a set of controlled inputs.

C.   The actual physical device that is running a mobile application.

D.   The identification of the real-world geographical location of a device.

4 REAL DEVICES, SIMULATORS, EMULATORS, AND THE CLOUD

The learning objectives for Chapter 4, Section 4, are:

MOB-4.4.1   (K2) Explain why testing is not conducted entirely on real devices.

MOB-4.4.2   (K3) For a given mobile testing project, determine how and when to use simulators/emulators during testing.

MOB-4.4.3   (K1) Recall how to verify the reliability of a simulator/emulator.

MOB-4.4.4   (K3) For a given mobile testing project, determine how and when to use cloud-based testing.

MOB-4.x.1   (K3) For a given mobile testing project, select the appropriate tools and environments for testing.

Let's return to this issue of the cubic meter of devices. How we can try to crack this nut? First, let's return to the obvious question: why can't we just test everything on real devices? Well, because it could involve a cubic meter of them, and that's really expensive. We'll look more closely at how expensive it is in a moment.

Nevertheless, the idea of using real devices is very appealing for us as testers. If test fidelity—the truthfulness of the test results in terms of similarity to production results—is the highest priority, the most important thing, then nothing comes near to tests run on real devices. You could say, "Look, let's minimize the risk of weird behaviors that escape from testing **and** contain test environment costs by restricting the list of supported devices to only those that we can afford to test on real devices in our test environment." However, in most places I've worked in, clients consulted with, and delivered training to—and trust me, that's thousands of organizations around the world—the tester tail just doesn't get to wag the sales and marketing dog.

Maybe you're lucky. Consider my retail client. They said, "It's iPhone only, we're not doing Android. We're not doing Android because there are too many different Android devices out there, and we can't customize for, build, deliver, and test them all. So, we'll standardize on iPhones." You might say that I'm contradicting my earlier comment about the testing tail not wagging the sales and marketing dog, but notice that they were looking at the whole development and maintenance process, not just testing.

My client was making an expensive decision in terms of production devices to purchase, because you can buy less expensive Android phones. However, this decision did save them time in terms of the testing and development. Remember, also, that any production failures that occur cost them money in terms of lost associate time, lost customers and so forth, which is different than the situation with most apps.

For the moment, let's just say we'll need to augment our test environment with simulators and emulators. However, this immediately raises the issue of test fidelity. How do we know that the simulator or emulator is giving us the right answer? We'll address that in a moment.

Are there other options, such as cloud-based services? Yes.

So, your test environment will probably consist of a mix of real devices, simulators, emulators, and cloud services.

Simulators and emulators vs real devices

It's not all downside with testing on simulators and emulators. Doing functional test automation on a real device can be a challenge, including tool availability. There can be issues with performance testing. Simulators and emulators make functional test automation and performance testing for mobile apps more practical.

Consider the following a basic rule of thumb for whether you need a real device. If you're testing usability, use a real device, especially if you're dealing with something like a game. Some of your performance testing needs to be done on real devices so you know how the quirks and limitations of the real devices affect app performance. Of course, any functional tests that are affected by some specific device quirk or feature of the device must be done on a real device.

Now, let's go back to this issue of test fidelity on simulators and emulators. The basic idea is to run some tests—identified through equivalence partitioning of the test conditions, for example—on both the real device and the simulator or emulator. For each test where the behavior is the same, you can trust the simulator or emulator to give valid results for that test and the ones like it; that is, in the same equivalence partition. For a test where the behavior is different, you can't trust the simulator or emulator for that test or those like it.

Another strategy is to be generous in your application of equivalence partitioning to identify different test environments. Don't identify every minor difference in a device as the need to have yet another configuration variation to cover. You have to do some analysis to figure out what a minor difference is, one that is unlikely to affect the way your app works. And you must remember that you're accepting a risk, and in some cases you'll be wrong about whether a difference really is minor.

So, let's return to this question of what a cubic meter of devices would cost, and do the math. Based on the size of a typical device, averaging out phones and tablets, there would be about 1,000 devices in a cubic meter. That's probably close to all possible configuration combinations, depending on what those configuration combinations are with respect to your app.

Be smart, though. If you use equivalence partitioning and pairwise techniques, maybe you can get down to a hundred configurations. In other words, don't try to actually buy the whole cubic meter of devices, but rather a subset that can adequately represent the cubic meter of devices. Further, some of those are just configuration variations on the same device, which we can handle by changing the configuration when we need to. So, let's assume we can get it down to 50 actual physical devices, each tested in two different configurations.

So, we have 50 devices, rather than the whole 1,000. Across all those tricks and techniques, we managed to eliminate 95 percent of the cubic meter of devices while still covering the entire set of configurations represented by the cubic meter of devices. Maybe that makes covering the cubic meter affordable?

I did some research, and the annual cost of ownership of a mobile device at the time of writing is around $2,000, including the wireless plan.[4] Now, if you don't have a wireless plan, you just pay for the device. But can you count on Wi-Fi to adequately represent what happens with the connectivity states and how they can affect your app? Remember, the whole point of the cubic meter of devices is to replicate, in every way, the physical client environment, so let's not skimp on the wireless plan. Fifty times $2,000, that's $100,000 a year for the devices alone.

Let's assume we plan for five hours of configuration-specific testing for every one of the 100 device configurations for every release, which is probably conservative. Further, let's plan for only four releases a year, which again is probably too low, but we'll use that for the calculations. This gives us 2,000 hours of device configuration testing per year.

---

[4] The specific internet websites that provide this information will change over time, as will this $2,000 figure. At the time of writing, a figure very close to $2,000 was available at the page here: https://www.wandera.com/about-wandera/wandera-in-the-media/press-archive/the-true-cost-of-mobility-u-s-enterprises-spending-1840-per-employee-mobile-device-annually/ However, by using "annual total cost of ownership mobile device" as a search string, you should be able to get an updated figure fairly quickly. Unless there is significant commoditization of mobile devices along with much greater competition in wireless carriers, it's hard to imagine this figure going down dramatically in the next three or four years. Of course, the total cost of ownership of a mobile device figure will be significantly different in other countries, as will the cost of labor.

How much does a typical hour of test labor cost? More research yields a typical figure of between $50 and $100 per hour. (This is what's referred to as the fully burdened labor rate, which takes into account the complete cost of the tester's time to the company, including benefits, office space, taxes, and so forth.) We'll use the $50 per hour figure. So, the device configuration testing costs $100,000, which is basically one full-time tester.[5]

For total cost, you're spending $100,000 on the devices themselves, and another $100,000 on the tester. That's $200,000 for the device-specific testing.

Now, in addition, you've got device-independent testing. This doesn't require any additional devices, since you've got plenty of devices. You can spread the device-independent testing across the 50 devices. However, this device-independent testing does involve more people.

In addition, you have to deal with this issue of managing these 50 devices, which includes some sort of test lab. That's a further cost. You also have loss of the devices that happens when they get dropped or sat on. You have the occasional unscrupulous contractor who accidentally puts a device in his case on the way out the door, and the tradesman who came in to paint a wall and left with a mobile device in his toolbox.

Summary: the cubic meter of devices, even when reduced by 95 percent to only 50,000 cubic centimeters of devices, is still really expensive.

So, what do we do if using real devices alone is not feasible? As I've already mentioned, simulators are one possibility. They have limitations as we saw earlier with the Android emulator, but they are useful. Further, many simulators are available for free from the platform vendors. Obviously, it's in the best interest of Google, Microsoft, and Apple to make sure that there are good simulators available for their app developers, because apps drive demand for the devices.

There is nothing magical about the simulators from the device vendors. If your team decided that the vendor simulators don't do what you need them to do, you could develop your own. However, that's no small effort.

Whatever the source of the simulator, it has to be verified. This involves running both functional and performance tests side by side, on a real device and the simulator, to ensure you get the same results.

Simulators will be necessary to do the performance and load testing on the server-side. For example, let's assume your app will be used by thousands of people at the same time, and these instances of your app will all communicate with the same server components. So, you need to know if your server components can scale, and whether your app will be fast enough under those levels of load. This involves simulating the incoming traffic of a thousand or more simultaneous users.

---

[5] You can find information on tester salaries here: www.payscale.com/research/US/Job=Software_Tester/Salary/b1aeb65b/ Entry-Level Remember that the salary to the tester doesn't take into account the other costs associated with having that employee, which will about double the cost.

Performance and load testing involves looking at throughput, response time, and resource utilization under load, as I mentioned before. However, there's something else that I recommend as part of a load test. As you use simulators to load the servers and test performance, in parallel, do a functional and usability test using a real device on the same servers. This allows you to check to see if usability and functionality degrade when the servers are loaded.

Emulators are somewhat more full-featured simulators. They replicate the capabilities of the device and the operating system more thoroughly than a simulator. The process of verifying an emulator and using it is basically the same as a simulator. As with simulators, it's important to keep track of the version.

For example, if there is a new release of the Android OS, and you're testing on Android devices, then you need to make sure that you're using the most recent version of the Android emulator.

In addition, you have to consider the learning curve for simulators and emulators. It's not dreadful, but it's certainly harder than testing your app on a real device. If you take a look at a typical simulator or emulator, you'll see they are complex pieces of software. Don't expect testers, especially non-technical ones, to simply start using a simulator or emulator for testing without some ramp up.

Cloud-based testing

In addition to simulators and emulators, you've also got cloud options. These are appliances and devices that can be used for testing. There are software agents that can simulate users, which is particularly helpful for your server-side testing. There are a number of vendors in this line of business.

Suppose you expect people connecting to and using your app from around the world. Those users connect to a set of servers in the United States. You'll need to test the experience for people connecting from across the world. For example, there can be some significant lag times in sending data to and from a device in New Zealand to a server in the US. For one thing, internet connectivity in that region, especially in New Zealand, is not that great anyway, and while you're communicating at the speed of light, it's still halfway around the world coming and halfway around the world going, so the round trip is literally a round-the-world distance. So, if you want to support the Australia/New Zealand market, you'll need to test that.

Network simulators can cover different kinds of network configurations and speed, and these are available as cloud resources, as are protocol simulators.

You'll need to ask yourself some key questions with these cloud-based testing resources. Will these resources support the kinds of performance and reliability tests you need to run? Will these cloud-based tests be realistic? Is access to the cloud-based resource convenient for you, including issues like the support facilities?

Security is a whole additional set of potential considerations. For example, if you're testing with actual production data, there can be personal identifying information in that production data. So, you have data anonymization issues that you need to deal with.

Disclosure of innovations can be a concern, too. Suppose you're creating an app that contains some particular new innovation, and you want to be first to market with this app that does this particular thing. If you use cloud-based testing resources, you're exposing the app to the outside world. Yes, people sign non-disclosure agreements but people also violate non-disclosure agreements.

The number of mobile app cloud testing options is amazing. Enter mobile app testing as a search string in your browser and it will explode with all these different options. Many of them are try-before-you-buy, which means that you can use it to do some testing of your app, and then decide whether to subscribe to or buy the service. These cloud options include real devices and simulators.

If you're going to use these cloud-based options, I recommend that, during the try-before-you-buy phase, shadow the testing that you're doing in this cloud testing option with some testing of real devices. Check to see whether the results that the cloud-based test vendor reports are the same as the results you're seeing. For example, if they tell you your app works just fine on the latest iPhone, run some tests on an iPhone. If you see different results, maybe this is not a trustworthy organization.

As I said, there are an incredible number of cloud testing options, which might make you feel overwhelmed. Maybe you decide to do some research on how to best select a cloud-based testing service provider. Be careful. While looking at the internet search results for cloud-based testing service providers, I noticed lots of articles and information about how to evaluate these service providers. Some of that material was written by people who worked at particular test labs, which is hardly an unbiased source.

You also have to be careful with industry analysts. For example, I've seen webinars advertised where the webinar is a joint effort by a tool vendor and one of the industry analyst companies. I've tuned into a few of these webinars, and most of them are basically infomercials.

So, be cautious. If someone is offering advice or help on selecting a testing service provider, or a tool vendor for that matter, check for conflicts of interest. Make sure they don't have a dog in the fight. This is one reason why my company, RBCS, is careful to avoid any such partnerships, because we want to provide our clients with unbiased advice.[6]

4.4 Test your knowledge

Let's try one or more sample exam questions related to the material we've just covered. The answers are found in Appendix C.

---

[6] For example, take a look at this recorded webinar on how to measure the performance of testing service providers: https://rbcs-us.com/resources/webinars/measuring-testing-service-providers/

Question 7 Learning objective: MOB-4.4.1 (K2) Explain why testing is not conducted entirely on real devices

Which of the following is an example of why not all mobile testing is performed on real devices?

    A.   realism of test results;

    B.   cost;

    C.   leakage of trade secrets;

    D.   browser availability.

Question 8 Learning objectives: MOB-4.4.2 (K3) For a given mobile testing project, determine how and when to use simulators/emulators during testing, MOB-4.4.4 (K3) For a given mobile testing project, determine how and when to use cloud-based testing, and MOB-4.x.1 (K3) For a given mobile testing project, select the appropriate tools and environments for testing. For a given mobile testing project, select the appropriate tools and environments for testing.

You are planning the testing of an application that must work on devices with many parallel applications running. The application must gather images and weather readings from devices accessible via the local area network and the internet, and process that data in real time. For the first release, your company intends to support Android devices only, as your main customer for the application has already standardized on Android smartphones and tablets.

Consider the following options for test tools and environments:

    i.   Android simulator;

    ii.   crowdsourced testers with their own devices;

    iii. iOS simulator;

    iv. cloud-hosted devices.

Consider the following test levels:

    A.   unit test;

    B.   system test;

    C.   Beta test.

Which of the following matches the tool or environment with the test levels in which that tool or environment will play a primary role?

    A.   A-I; B-IV; C-II;

    B.   A-I, III; B-IV; C-II;

    C.   A-II; B-I, II, III; C-IV;

    D.   A-II; B-IV; C-II.

Question 9 Learning objective: MOB-4.4.3 (K1) Recall how to verify the reliability of a simulator/emulator

How can you verify the reliability of a simulator for functional testing?

    A.   check with the vendor;

    B.   avoid open-source simulators;

    C.   generate large volumes of user input;

    D.   compare real device behavior.

APPLY YOUR KNOWLEDGE

Now, work through an exercise related to the material we've just covered. An example solution is found in Appendix B.

This exercise is a continuation of the previous exercise, and it's about making provision decisions. In this exercise, you'll decide how much of your testing you want to do on real devices. Further, for those devices, you'll decide how many you want to own and how many you want to test via crowdsourcing, remote device labs, or open device labs. You'll also decide on the use of simulators, emulators, and cloud-based options, in terms of which tests you plan to run on those. In other words, in this exercise, you'll outline the device-side of your test environment.

If you are working in a group, discuss your solution with others after you complete it.

5 PERFORMANCE TEST TOOLS AND SUPPORT

The learning objectives for Chapter 4, Section 5, are:

MOB-4.5.1   (K2) Explain how the cloud can be used to support performance testing.

MOB-4.5.2   (K2) Explain the types of data a performance tool needs to be able to create and track.

MOB-4.x.1   (K3) For a given mobile testing project, select the appropriate tools and environments for testing.

For performance testing, there are some specific things we need to be aware of, including ways to use tools, cloud resources and different types of data, so in this section we'll take a look at these topics.

In terms of tools, as with mobile test automation in general, you have many different options. A search of the internet for mobile performance testing or mobile performance test tools will turn up hundreds of options, including commercial and open source.

Some of these are traditional performance testing tools that have been extended to mobile. It makes sense to have some healthy skepticism of such tools, because that's kind of similar to the test management tools that claim to support both waterfall and Agile life cycles. What my clients tell me about those situations is that, if you're using a traditional test management tool in an Agile environment, there are challenges because the tool was developed with a sequential life cycle model in mind and it's not really well suited to Agile. On the flip side, the other thing I hear is that people who use Agile task management tools, even with supposed test management add-ons, find their experience is not very good, either, because the tools are well-suited to Agile, but feel like they were created by people who had limited experience of managing test projects.

So, I would be concerned that an extended traditional performance testing tool that also tries to be in the mobile world might not be very capable. But, on the other side, the specialized performance mobile tools are likely to be relatively new, and perhaps not stable or reliable. The moral here, as always, is that, in tool selection of any kind, be really careful.

An essential element in a performance tool is the ability to generate realistic load. Realistic load is load that looks like what will actually happen—what will actually be coming into your app or coming into your server from your app.

This brings us back to use cases and the mix of use cases at any given time. This concept of realistic use cases and a realistic likely mix of use cases is referred to as an operational profile. However, for realism in performance testing of mobile apps, given the diversity of the users, personas are part of the puzzle, too, as we discussed in the previous chapter.

If you're generating load that does not look like what the real world will dish up, your performance test results are misleading. The number one question when you're thinking about a performance testing tool is whether it can generate realistic load.

Realistic loads are not constant. Load varies, based on things like time of day, day of the week, and sometimes even monthly or seasonal variations. For example, if you're in retail, you'll see a lot of seasonal variations. If you offer tax services, there are a few months in the year when things really heat up.

Traditionally, acquiring performance test tools meant having something on your premises. Now you also have cloud-based providers, including for mobile performance testing. This might be a better way to do the performance testing for your app, because such a provider might be able to better simulate geographical diversity. In addition, it could be more affordable, depending on how often you need to do performance testing, because instead of buying an expensive tool, you're renting it.

If you do need to buy a tool, you definitely need to think about future needs, but even if you use an outsourced testing service provider, think about the future. It's better to establish a relationship with a testing service provider and keep that relationship over a period of time, rather than starting over at the beginning of every project.

Some people say that forcing testing service providers to compete for the business at the start of every project ensures that you choose the best provider, but I would say that it actually just increases the percentage of time you'll spend using the wrong providers. Why? Because, rather than stick with an established relationship with a testing service provider you can trust, you open yourself up to choosing a company with a good sales operation and poor ability to deliver the service. Further, when you go back to the original service provider, the one you could have trusted, now they are likely to assign less important staff to your projects, because you have become a less important and untrustworthy customer. A testing service provider you can count on that does good work is not a relationship to be thrown away lightly.

Performance testing loads often consist of a complex mix of data flows, so we need to know what's flowing with your performance test tool. There are data from the device to the server and the server to the device, which is a mix of data associated with the use cases and personas discussed earlier. This mix of data must be carefully designed. There are volume and frequency issues you have to take into account, as I mentioned.

As one reviewer of this book mentioned regarding load testing data flows, devices can have limits on the number of messages they can receive at once, including system messages related to connectivity loss and reestablishment. So, it's important to stress test the device as well as the server.

With mobile testing, you have to consider patterns of connections, disconnections, and reconnections. The traditional approach to performance testing in the client–server world is to simulate dozens, hundreds, or thousands of clients, all pounding away over the network on the servers. However, that doesn't model the mobile reality of connections dropping, being retried, and being reestablished. It also doesn't model the throttling of data flows that occurs as signal strength and connection type change.

You also have to model burstiness of load. While "burstiness" may not be an actual word, it refers to situations where large bursts of data are followed by periods of no data flowing at all. Remember my earlier example of a newsfeed app that allows you to subscribe to certain newsfeeds so you get breaking news? Consider the data flows that happen when there is a tsunami, or when some politician gives a big speech, or there's a Fed announcement. In such situations, you get a big burst of data, but that's followed by periods where there's no data flowing at all.

As I mentioned, your tool must give you the ability to simulate a realistic set of transactions given the variations associated with time of day, day of week, seasonality, and so forth, along with variations associated with business versus personal use. For example, if you were performance testing the Twitter app, during business hours, you have a certain number of people that use Twitter from a business perspective, and they use it in a certain way. Outside business hours, the usage is primarily personal, which is another way of using the app.

As I said, realism of generated load is definitely an important requirement. Equally important is the ability to measure performance metrics that actually matter to you. You have to look at both load generation and performance measurement.

Let's again look at the Adler app, shown in Figure 4.5, as an example.

For this app, there are both client-side performance issues and server-side performance issues, both of which we have to consider. You need to think about how to generate realistic load and how to take meaningful measurements. Remember that the tools will tend to have default measurements, and perhaps quite a few of them, but you have to be careful of those default measurements. These can result in a situation where you have too much information, with a lot of it that's not relevant. This is nowhere near as useful as exactly the right information you need.

That may seem like an obvious statement, but I bring it up because I see this a lot. I see people that do performance testing, whether they're using a tool or outsourcing it, and they're not bringing performance engineering and performance testing expertise to that process, so they tend to make a lot of mistakes.

Figure 4.5 The main menu of the Adler airlines app

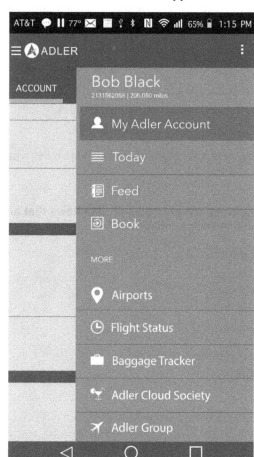

So, with this app, some of the performance testing I might do with a tool and some of it I might do with a cloud-based service. If I were responsible for testing the Adler app, I'd probably want to do some amount of cloud-based testing, since I'd want to simulate travelers from around the world. For example, think of the customers in the Australia/ New Zealand region, the scenario I brought up before. What if I'm on an Adler partner flight; I'm in New Zealand or Australia, and I need to get on the app via Wi-Fi to make some changes or check flight status. What is the users' experience with that?

4.5 Test your knowledge

Let's try one or more sample exam questions related to the material we've just covered. The answers are found in Appendix C.

Question 10 Learning objective: MOB-4.5.1 (K2) Explain how the cloud can be used to support performance testing

How would you use the cloud for performance testing a mobile application's server-side components?

    A.   rent cloud protocol simulators;
    B.   rent cloud-hosted agents;
    C.   check the emulator against real devices;
    D.   generate load according to operational profiles.

Question 11 Learning objective: MOB-4.5.2 (K2) Explain the types of data a performance tool needs to be able to create and track

Which TWO of the following are examples of data flows that are specific to performance and/or reliability testing a mobile app?

    A.   transaction data;
    B.   GPS information;
    C.   images;
    D.   activity bursts;
    E.   peak usage level.

6 TEST AUTOMATION

The learning objective for Chapter 4, Section 6, is:

MOB-4.x.1   (K3) For a given mobile testing project, select the appropriate tools and environments for testing.

In this final section for Chapter 4, we talk about test automation, and primarily I'm referring to functional test automation. If you've worked in Agile life cycles for any length of time, you know that rapid change brings with it increased regression risk. The usual way to manage regression risk is with automated functional regression tests. Ideally, these are part of your continuous integration framework.

Mobile development is often even more intensive, with a lot of pressure to get stuff out quickly. The paradox is that the time pressures and rapid change make it a real challenge to get good automated tests in place, due to resource issues and time constraints.

I've previously mentioned a classic mistake of automation, using a bad automation tool selection process. Another classic mistake that I hear about all the time is bad test engineer selection process. Here's how that conversation usually goes:

I ask a client, "How are you doing your automated testing?"

They say, "Well, we're really busy, but we've got these two new hires that are fresh out of college. They've got computer science degrees, and they know how to program. We're having them head up our test automation effort."

In response, I say, "Look, there's really not a very nice way of saying this, so I'll just say it: that's very unlikely to work. Those people don't know what they're doing. Test automation is a complicated thing. A lot of mistakes can be made, and unless someone has been involved in test automation for a long time, they are very unlikely to know what those mistakes are, which makes it really difficult to avoid them."

Do yourself and your organization a favor. If you embark on an automation effort, take the tool selection process very seriously and have somebody leading the effort who has at least five years of functional test automation experience, ideally with the same type of tool that you're using. If their experience involves automating through a command line interface, and you're now trying to automate through a mobile device graphical user interface, some of that experience is transferable but some is not.

General observations on good automated tests

An experienced test automation person will know how to recognize good automated tests, including the critical consideration associated with maintaining those automated tests. Let me mention a few of the attributes of good automated tests.

To start with, good automated tests often realistically simulate actual usage. Automated tests should cover the way the user interacts with the device, and possibly in a way that looks like a typical use case. The test should check whether the task was done and whether it was done in a way that would be acceptable for users.

Good automated tests will also ideally cover the way your app causes the supported devices to interact with the server-side. Basically, this means you want full end-to-end tests as part of your automated test suite. By end-to-end tests, I mean a test that starts some activity on the client-side that makes something happen on the server-side and includes evaluating whether what happened on the server-side was correct. For example, suppose I use the Adler mobile app to book a flight, and I get a message on the app that says the flight's been booked. Okay, great, but I still need to go to the website and verify that the reservation is there. Alternatively, I could go directly to the database, if my automation tool is set up that way, and have the tool query the reservation data from the database.

Maintainability of automated tests is critical too. The classic approach over the last 20 years or so to creating maintainable functional test automation scripts is to use either data-driven or keyword-driven architectures. I've been using data-driven and keyword-driven architectures for automation since 1992. These approaches have been around quite a while. You can use these architectures for API testing, graphical user interface testing, command line interface testing, report-based testing, and more. The basic idea in both approaches is to insulate the test scripts from the user interface through modularity, and to separate the test scripts from the test cases themselves.

However you approach it, definitely think about maintenance. The classic sad story, which I've heard from all too many clients and is the stage four cancer diagnosis of test automation, is when a client says to me, "We don't have time to create any new tests anymore because we're busy maintaining the tests that we've already created."

I have heard that over and over again. It's never a fixable situation. It is a true example of having painted yourself well and fully into a corner. You have a large suite of unmaintainable automated tests. Guess what? All of them must be thrown away. You'll need to start over.

When someone objects and says, "But we've invested so much into these tests, and they are yielding valuable results," keep in mind the economic concept of the sunk cost fallacy.[7] Whatever you do, don't get into this fix.

Easy to say, "huh? How to do that, though?" Also easy to say: treat test automation projects as software development projects. Use proper configuration management, ideally in the same repository as the app you're testing. Follow good coding practices, whatever scripting or programming languages you're using. Use an actual life cycle, whether sequential, Agile, or spiral; I've used each of those three life cycles to successfully implement automated tests. Have code reviews for the test scripts. Test the test scripts and the tests themselves as they are built.

It's also useful to remember, in test automation, if you can't get the whole loaf, half a loaf may very well do. There's no shame in automating through the simulator and emulator and getting as much functional testing done there as you can, then augmenting that with some manual regression testing on real devices.

Test automation tools

As with performance tools, you've got a lot of options for mobile functional test automation tools. Your options include commercial and open-source solutions, along with building your own custom tool. Some of the tools are mobile-specific, while others are extended traditional tools. The same comments I made in the previous section about performance tools would apply here.

---

[7] Read this article by Tejvan Pettinger (2017) for a description of the sunk cost fallacy: www.economicshelp.org/blog/27047/economics/sunk-cost-fallacy/

With any tool, as I've said before, know your requirements and select the tool based on well understood requirements that at least have been reviewed and approved by a wide number of stakeholders. Ideally, the requirements themselves were gathered from a wide number of stakeholders. The tool requirements and constraints should be influenced by your test environment choices, but it's also true that your tool choices should influence your environment choices.

As I've said previously about performance test tools, an automated test can make data flow to the servers and to other devices. So, don't rely entirely on the app's user interface when evaluating expected results, but actually check that it did indeed work and that the data went where it was supposed to go. Sometimes, that can be done by just putting extensions on an existing tool that allow it to do database queries on a remote database. There are often ways to make that work, though sometimes it involves a little coding.

To reiterate, the selection of the test automator or automated test engineer is one of the most critical decisions in the project, as critical as the selection of the right tool. To me, this means at least five years of test automation experience in the lead person. Programming skills and scripting skills are essential.

How important is a mobile focus for the automators? Could you bring someone in who had five years of test automation experience using a GUI test automation tool on PCs? You probably could move that person into a lead automator role for a mobile app, assuming you plan to test through the graphical user interface, but there would be some learning curve.

It would be better to have somebody with more knowledge of mobile test tools, mobile devices, mobile apps, mobile cloud testing options, and so forth. In other words, someone who is already a mobile geek. It takes some exposure to mobile apps and mobile testing before the realization hits that, yes, this is actually substantially different than testing PC apps.

Keyword-driven test automation

Let's go into a bit more detail on keyword-driven test automation. The keywords are very similar to your use case names because they're some sort of business process. The keywords can define either coarse-grained or fine-grained interactions. This granularity is an important decision, which we'll return to in a moment.[8]

The keywords are from the user point of view, which allows the tester to write tests using the keywords. Suppose, for example, I'm testing an ecommerce app, and I want to make a purchase. So, part of that could involve the use of a select item keyword, which corresponds to the user at a screen that's showing some items, then clicking on a given item, and ultimately selecting the number and possibly color and size of the item. Now, the postcondition is that the item is in my cart.

---

[8] For a more detailed description of keyword-driven test automation and this example in particular, see my 2015 book, written with Jamie Mitchell, *Advanced Software Testing: Volume 3* (second edition 2015, San Rafael, CA: Rocky Nook). I thank Jamie for his contributions in that book to this example, which I'm summarizing here.

In keyword-driven testing, the tests are composed of rows of keywords in a table, often a spreadsheet or XML file or something like that. Each test starts with a keyword, in this example "select item", in the first column. In the following columns are the data items that go with that keyword, such as the item name or item ID, the number, the color, and the size, with the expected results to be checked in a final column.

Table 4.1 A simple keyword table

Keyword	Data1	Data2	Result
Add_User	User1	Pass1	User added message
Add_User	@Rec34	@Rec35	User added message
Reset_Password	User1	Welcome	Password reset confirmation message
Delete_User	User1		Invalid username/password message
Add_User	User3	Pass3	User added message
Delete_User	User2		User not found message

Table 4.1 shows an example of a very simple keyword table, for account management. We have the keyword in the first column of the table, and we then have up to two pieces of data, "data1" and "data2." This is a simplified example, and you can have "data3," "data4," "data5," "data6," as many columns as you need to accommodate the maximum number of data items used by a particular keyword.

Finally, you have the expected result. This is a fairly simple expected result. It can be more complicated, looking at screenshots and those sort of things.

Notice in some rows we have the data provided directly, as in the first row with "User1" and "Pass1." We can also have data by reference, using the @ sign, such as @Rec34 and @Rec35 in the second row, which allows you to refer to some other part of the table that has the data, which can be useful.

If you look at the "delete" row, you see a keyword with a single data item.

The way this all works is that you have a master script that reads the table row by row. It reads the keyword and it recognizes that the keyword corresponds to a particular automation script or sequence of scripts. It invokes that first script.

Usually, if you're testing via a GUI, each screen has its own script. That way, if any one screen changes, you change the script that handles that screen, which automatically propagates the change to all the tests that use that script. In other words, you only have to make one script change per screen change.

This addresses one of the classic brittleness problems with automation, which is where every script goes through all the screens involved in a single test, and, when one screen changes, every single script that goes through that screen has to change.

Keyword-driven architecture is a very flexible and maintainable approach. As I said, it can be used not only for testing through the graphical user interface, but also for testing through a command line interface or application program interfaces.

Keyword granularity

There are a number of considerations for keyword-driven testing. Let's start by returning to this issue of keyword granularity.

There are good reasons to make the keywords more fine-grained. The more fine-grained you get, the more you can use the keywords as building blocks, and in more flexible ways.

For example, if we're testing an ecommerce app, I could have a keyword that corresponded to making a purchase, right from starting at the home page, all the way through to seeing the confirmation screen. However, that's too coarse-grained and needs to be broken down into smaller pieces.

A better keyword granularity would be to have a browsing keyword, an account creation keyword, an account maintenance keyword, a logging in keyword, an item selection keyword, an edit card keyword, an enter purchase method keyword, an enter shipping address keyword, a confirm order keyword, and so on.

As you can see, this more fine-grained approach to defining the keywords gives you building blocks that can be used to create a lot of different tests. However, fine-grained keywords can have script maintenance complexity issues. For example, you have to keep track of the relationships between keywords and the scripts that go with each particular screens, so the larger the number of keywords, the more complex those relationships might be.

Another consideration is whether you want keywords for low-level actions, such as changing a configuration value or an operating system setting that affects the way your application works. Obviously, that's a nice feature that allows more testing power, but from a test maintenance point of view it creates the possibility that changes to the way Android or iOS work can ripple through and break your tests, incurring a hard-to-anticipate test maintenance activity.

Forward thinking

In addition to the need for careful initial keyword design, remember that you need to be able define new keywords and new scripts as the screens change and evolve. So, maintainability also means the ability to add and change keywords and scripts.

Also understand that keyword-driven test automation is focused on the long term. So, the breakeven point may seem far away when you're going through all this process of building the keywords, scripts, programs, tests, data, and so forth. There will be a fair amount of work before you're able to achieve any significant test coverage, and it can be tempting to skimp on design to get some quick wins on the board.

Resist that temptation. Keep in mind that the only way to get a positive return on investment in test automation is to make a real investment. What I've seen over and over again with clients is that, when they take shortcuts and use unproven, unmaintainable architectures, they often have an illusion of immediate positive return of investment, but that eventually becomes negative as the costs of maintenance mount.

4.6 Test your knowledge

Let's try one or more sample exam questions related to the material we've just covered. The answers are found in Appendix C.

Question 12 Learning objective: recall of syllabus content only (K1)

Traditional test automation techniques are not useful for mobile application testing.

  A. This statement is wrong, and keyword-driven approaches are an example.
  B. This statement is true, and in fact test automation is not important for mobile apps.
  C. This statement is true for mobile applications with server-side components.
  D. This statement is wrong, because exploratory testing is useful for mobile apps.

APPLY YOUR KNOWLEDGE

Now, work through an exercise related to the material we've just covered. An example solution is found in Appendix B.

Continuing on with your chosen application, this exercise involves defining a set of keywords. First, determine the main use cases. Next, decide on the proper level of granularity.

Now, define a keyword table, like the one shown in Table 4.1. Try to exercise the major functional areas of your app.

If you are working in a group, discuss your solution with others after you complete it.

In this chapter, we addressed two key differences between mobile app testing and other kinds of software testing, environments, and tools. In our discussion of tools, we also covered tools for performance testing and functional test automation. In the sections on test environments, we addressed how the type of mobile app you're testing affects your test environment needs and how you can assemble a mix of test environment resources that will address your testing needs while staying within your budgetary constraints.

5   FUTURE-PROOFING

In this final, brief chapter, we address what's coming towards us in the mobile app testing world, at ever increasing speed. The mobile world will grow rapidly, so we must build flexibly, and be ready to change. We must plan for the future and we must try to see around corners as the future comes towards us.

CHAPTER SECTIONS

Chapter 5, Future-Proofing, contains the following four sections

1. Expect rapid growth
2. Build for change
3. Plan for the future
4. Anticipating the future

CHAPTER TERMS

There are no terms to remember for Chapter 5.

1 EXPECT RAPID GROWTH

The learning objectives for Chapter 5, Section 1, are:

MOB-5.1.1   (K1) Recall ways in which the mobile application and device market will expand.

MOB-5.1.2   (K1) Recall areas in which user expectations will increase.

For the foreseeable future, expect rapid expansion of apps, devices, and user expectations. As mentioned in the previous chapter, there are already around six million mobile apps across all the different platforms. As long as the vendors find ways to avoid the dreaded commoditization trap by adding new features and as long as users are willing to pay extra money for snazzy new features like heart rate monitors and who knows what next, you will see continued expansion. As long as money grows on the mobile trees, new vendors will enter the market and partnerships of various kinds will be formed with traditional vendors and traditional brands.

For example, if you are so inclined—and sufficiently wealthy—you can buy an Apple Watch that was made in partnership with Hermés, the famous French company. So, you have a luxury brand that teams up with a technology company, with some interesting testing implications. As another example, consider the Vertu luxury mobile phones, some of which cost over $10,000 and feature things like titanium cases and so forth. Imagine if a large percentage of your customer base consists of people who spend over $1,000 on a smart watch or over $10,000 on a fancy mobile phone, both of which will be technologically obsolete in two years.

The app makers are getting ever cleverer about getting and keeping people's attention, so people are constantly using their devices. This means that expectations about reliability, usability, and performance will only go up.

We will probably also see the reality of—and people's expectations of—a convergence in the look and feel of mobile apps. For example, consider that, in the early days of ecommerce, Amazon pretty much set the standard for how ecommerce is supposed to work, and if you tried to do something that was very different, unless it offered noticeable advantages to the customer, that would be resisted.

Not only are device vendors trying to avoid commoditization, but app makers also must fight harder and harder to try to distinguish themselves as well, so features are added quickly and fixing bugs immediately is the order of the day.

So, user expectations are high already and those expectations will only get higher. What we have to do, as testers, is to try to understand and cover those expectations as much as we possibly can within constraints.

5.1 Test your knowledge

Let's try one or more sample exam questions related to the material we've just covered. The answers are found in Appendix C.

Question 1 Learning objective: MOB-5.1.1 (K1) Recall ways in which the mobile application and device market will expand

Which of the following statements is true?

    A. Mobile apps will increase but devices will decrease.

    B. Mobile apps and mobile devices will remain stable.

    C. Mobile apps will remain stable whilst devices will increase.

    D. Mobile apps and mobile devices will increase.

Question 2 Learning objective: MOB-5.1.2 (K1) Recall areas in which user expectations will increase

In the future, users of mobile applications will:

    A.   Tolerate slow releases as long as the quality is high.

    B.   Expect software that's better, delivered faster.

    C.   Be happy with faster, reliable apps, even if the behavior is inconsistent.

    D.   Move back to using PC and internet apps.

2 BUILD FOR CHANGE

The learning objectives for Chapter 5, Section 2, are:

MOB-5.2.1   (K2) Summarize the considerations for building a flexible testing framework.

MOB-5.2.2   (K4) Analyze a given mobile testing project and determine the appropriate activities to reduce maintenance costs while enabling wide product adoption.

Faster, better, cheape—back in the late 1990s, the head of NASA, Dan Goldin, pushed this concept. I've always scoffed at that with the response, "Sure. Pick two." There were some NASA missions that went very well, but there were also some missions that flopped, such as a couple of failed Mars missions.

Like it or not, in mobile apps for the near future, due to the competition, the need to stay relevant, and the need to avoid becoming a commodity, faster, better, cheaper is a reality we'll have to live in. So, you need to find ways to use tools, automation, and good automation architectures. You'll need to make smart decisions about buying versus renting tools and environments. As one reviewer of this book mentioned, this also means being as involved as possible in project planning so you can plan your testing accordingly.

You'll need to keep your skills sharp, so that you are as efficient as possible. After all, if you're in a faster, better, cheaper kind of world, efficiency is really the name of the game, more so than effectiveness. A good job done in a day will beat a perfect job done in a week, and an okay job done in an hour beats the good job done in a day.

What does this mean to us as testers? Well, if we can get to 75 percent coverage or just 50 percent coverage in two days, but it will take a month to get to 100 percent, we have to go for the 75 percent or even the 50 percent. That's a tough pill to swallow. Many times, as testers, we want to champion a philosophy that proclaims there ain't no substitute for doing it right. As much as I would love to be able to hold to that, I think for certain mobile apps you'll find that there is a substitute for doing it right, which is doing it okay and quickly.

It depends on what you're working on. If you're working on a safety-critical application where, if that application gives bad information or makes a bad thing happen, somebody will die, then faster, better, cheaper is not a good motto. However, faster, better, cheaper does apply to you if you're making a disposable app that will be around for six months or so. These things come and go like pollen, so do you really want to sweat the last detail of quality? Probably not.

However, there **are** certainly mobile devices where you would sweat the last detail of quality. For example, do you want a faster, better, cheaper pacemaker implanted in your chest? I have clients that work in the FDA-regulated world, and they're not the faster, better, cheaper types. If I said, "Faster, better, cheaper," to them, they would look at me like I had two heads.

How to build for change

Part of building for change is having a flexible test architecture.[1] Think Lego®. A flexible test architecture is Lego®-like, and consists of test components that are Lego®-like. This means things like many small scripts can be snapped together to do many different things.

Part of this will be enabled by having the right tools, so again I'll stress the need to be very careful with tool selection. As I've mentioned, I've seen many times that sloppy, hurried tool selection was the first chapter in a sad story about how, in some cases, over a million dollars was wasted on automation that didn't work out.

Flexible test architectures are also enabled by test maintainability. Don't take shortcuts on maintainability, either. Use people who have the skills and the smarts. Also, try to use people who have done it before, in the sense that they've built automation solutions and environments in the technological and business spaces that you're working in.

Be smart and have a "just diverse enough" environment. What I mean here is that you use real devices where you have to, but avoid drowning in the cubic meter of devices.

Use risk-based testing to make sure that you are focused on the most important coverage areas, as described earlier in this book. As one of the reviewers of this book mentioned, make sure you are using risk-based testing appropriately, based on the type of app you're testing and the risks associated with it.

Look for ways to take advantage of crowdsourcing, testing in the wild, and testing in production, but carefully manage any business or quality risks associated with those options. (As an example of what I mean by quality risks, keep in mind that, in some cases, such as a safety-critical app that controls an insulin pump, such testing may border on criminally reckless.) For example, when testing in production, you can use what's called A/B testing. In A/B testing, there are features that are out there and they're available on your server, but only a small percentage of your users actually see them. You set up your app to select certain users (but not all) based on certain characteristics of their use and expose them to new features. You evaluate their response to the new features, and decide based on that whether to roll the features out to more users, and see how that works.

---

[1] Some good information on flexible test architectures can be found at: www.istqb.org/component/jdownloads/send/48-advanced-level-test-automation-engineer-documents/201-advanced-test-automation-engineer-syllabus-ga-2016.html

As I said, efficiency is king in the faster, better, cheaper world. So, know your testing return on investment and your automation return on investment, and look for ways to optimize those. It will be less about effectiveness and more about efficiency when you're time-squeezed, unless you're in the safety-critical world.

Further, when you're thinking about investment in various test assets such as tools, automated tests, environments, data, and so forth, consider the app. If you are in the business of building disposable apps that are intended to be a flash in the pan, something people use for about six months or so before moving on to something else, spending a lot of money creating a really sophisticated test automation system for such an app is foolish.

So, for such apps, look for the quick and cheap not the slow and perfect. Now, that said, whilst the test automation part might not be a good place to invest, your environments and tools might be things you want to invest in, assuming that those will transfer from the current disposable app to the next one.

A recurring theme in this book is that you must be really careful in your selection of your test tools, your test partners, and your testing service providers. There are good discussions of tool selection criteria in the ISTQB® Certified Tester Foundation syllabus and the Advanced Test Manager syllabus 2012 which can provide guidance in this regard.[2]

In addition to the factors discussed in those documents, you need to keep in mind that things are moving more rapidly in the mobile world. This means that vendor and/or open-source community responsiveness and tool flexibility should figure high on your priority list when you put your requirements together. And I do mean this literally, in that you should have a prioritized requirements list as part of your tool selection process.

Another consideration, as I mentioned, is the expected app lifetime. If you're building a throwaway app, use a throwaway test automation approach. Perhaps a quick set of automated tests running through a simulator gets you some decent benefit, quickly.

So, you can compromise some of your requirements on the tools and compromise on your automation goals, if it's a matter of urgency and kind of a throwaway situation. However, in terms of vendors, partners and so forth, you want long-term relationships with trusted partners that value you as a business partner.

Here's something to keep in mind about testing service providers and tool vendors of all sorts. When you're evaluating these companies, sometimes organizations take the viewpoint that big is better. They want to use some huge company with a huge name that is a market leader in terms of revenue.

However, before you do this, consider the amount of business that you will do with them. In order for you to be an important customer to one of the top ten testing service or tools companies, you must do millions and millions of dollars of business with them every year. If that's not your budget, you'll never be a really important client to them.

---

[2] For more details, see my 2012 book *Foundations of Software Testing* (Cengage: Boston, MA), with Dorothy Graham and Erik van Veenendaal, and my 2009 book *Advanced Software Testing: Volume 2* (second edition 2014, San Rafael, CA: Rocky Nook).

This means that the company won't assign its top talent, its star players, to your projects or account. If it later happens that one of the people they assign to your projects grows into a star player, that person will probably be moved to another project or account. So, if you intend to spend a limited amount of money, the small to mid-size providers might be a better choice, if you're looking to get a testing service provider.

Now, that same rule doesn't always apply exactly to tool selection. A smaller tool vendor might be willing to work harder to earn your money and they might be willing to be more responsive to your needs. However, you have to balance that against the possibility that the smaller tool vendor will go out of business.

For both service providers and tool vendors, you'll want to examine their track record, including how responsive they have been to change and how they've handled disruptive technologies. For example, you might ask them, "Suppose the wearables mobile market catches fire tomorrow and we start focusing on apps for those platforms, explain how you could move quickly enough to help us test such apps."

Let's look at an example of the old saying that the perfect is the enemy of the good. Suppose I have two potential approaches to automation. One will allow me to address 75 percent of my coverage goals; it's a GUI and keyword-driven approach, and it's something that will be maintainable for years. The other only gets to 25 percent of my coverage goals, and works through APIs and the data layer.

Now, if these are the same cost, require the same effort, and have the same breakeven point, I will take the first one. However, what if I can go through the API and data layer and have that done in a third of the time or less? This is not a purely hypothetical question, because API automation is relatively easy, tends to be relatively maintainable, and allows access to a lot of the business functionality through APIs in many cases. So, that might be good enough.

It's also possible that you don't do either; you do both. This exact situation came up with a client a while back. What I told them was to attack part of the test automation problem through the API and get what they could that way. Then, attack another part of the test automation problem through reports comparisons, which is basically going to the data layer, and testing through reports is relatively easy too. Once they had those two quick and cheap partial coverage approaches in place, they should look at what they hadn't covered and think about a keyword-driven approach that allowed them to achieve the rest of their coverage goals over a longer period.

5.2 Test your knowledge

Let's try one or more sample exam questions related to the material we've just covered. The answers are found in Appendix C.

Question 3 Learning objective: MOB-5.2.1 (K2) Summarize the considerations for building a flexible testing framework

To allow for change in the future, you should:

A. Focus your test architecture using risk analysis.
B. Focus on functional test automation.
C. Focus on non-functional test automation.
D. Expect a positive ROI only in the very long term.

Question 4 Learning objective: MOB-5.2.2 (K4) Analyze a given mobile testing project and determine the appropriate activities to reduce maintenance costs while enabling wide product adoption

You are planning the testing of an application that must work on devices with many parallel applications running. The application must gather images and weather readings from devices accessible via the local area network and the internet, and process that data in real time. For the first release, your company intends to support Android devices only, as your main customer for the application has already standardized on Android smartphones and tablets.

Which of the following should be part of your strategy for reducing test environment maintenance costs?

A. Purchase all supported Android devices but no iOS or other smartphone devices.
B. Focus on testing Android smartphones, as tablets are less likely to have problems.
C. Buy one of each supported data-providing device for your in-house test network.
D. Exploit cloud-based devices for most compatibility testing.

APPLY YOUR KNOWLEDGE

Now, work through an exercise related to the material we've just covered. An example solution is found in Appendix B.

For your chosen app, outline some of the things you can do that will lead to a higher level of long-term test maintainability. You should address issues such as:

- How you will manage your skills as a tester?

- How you will do good tool selection?

- How you will handle partner and vendor selection?

- What is the best approach to designing tests and documenting them?

- How will you keep test information in your test management system?

If you are working in a group, discuss your solution with others.

3 PLAN FOR THE FUTURE

The learning objective for Chapter 5, Section 3, is:

MOB-5.3.1 (K2) Explain how life cycle models are likely to change and how this will affect testing.

Software engineering has experienced a number of big trends, to the point where the Gartner analysts have created something called the hype cycle. If you've never seen the hype cycle, a quick search on the internet will locate it.[3] It's an easy-to-understand concept, which says that trends start small, but then reach a point where they get hyped all out of proportion to what they actually offer. Ultimately, the hype subsides and the trend—whatever it was—becomes absorbed into the general way software engineering is done.

Here's an example of a software engineering hype cycle. In the late 1980s and early 1990s, object-oriented programming became a major force. Some people said and wrote that object-oriented programming would create a world where we would have huge collections of pre-tested objects, written in C++ or some other similar object-oriented language. These pre-tested objects would be like common civil engineering materials, such as I-beams, concrete, steel plates, asphalt, and so forth. Software engineering would become a simple matter of snapping these together, assembling them like building blocks or Lego®, to build whatever you want.

Since these were all going to be pre-tested objects, all of our quality problems would disappear. Since these would be handy building blocks available to everyone, productivity would go through the roof.

Well, none of that happened. Consider that Microsoft Windows 10 is written in large part in C++. I would not hold that up as a paragon of quality. What we saw was that the reality of object-oriented software did not live up to the hype.

In *Software Testing Techniques* (1990),[4] Boris Beizer made a joke about this kind of thinking. The title of the section in the book is, in Latin, the language will be our savior, thus poking fun at the quasi-religious levels of fervor that have surrounded such fads.

If this were an isolated incident, it would be an amusing anecdote but there'd be little to learn from it. However, it's not isolated, but rather is just a particularly large example of something that happens all the time. Fourth generation languages were another example of a language fad.

Total Quality Management and Six Sigma are two more examples of ideas that became fads, though I know that there are very valuable concepts in both of them. In the 1990s, the Software Engineering Institute took ideas from Total Quality Management, especially the idea that the quality of the product arises from the quality of the process. So, they created an approach to building software, expressed in the Capability Maturity Model or

---

[3] As of the time of writing, you can find the hype cycle here: www.gartner.com/smarterwithgartner/top-trends-in-the-gartner-hype-cycle-for-emerging-technologies-2017/
[4] New York: Van Nostrand Reinhold.

CMM, that is focused on implementing best practices of software engineering through-out the software process.

Some people might see Agile as a reaction against the approach expressed in CMM and its successor CMMI. However, it's really an affirmation of the core belief that getting the process right is central to software success. To rephrase Beizer's aphorism, software engineering is in the grips of a long-term fixation on process as the savior.

However, life cycle processes continue to change, with Kanban and DevOps the emerging ideas now. These process changes include good ideas and bad ideas. Often, one of the main drivers behind these changes is accelerating the delivery of software. Back when Agile was emerging as a major force, I remember closely questioning some executives at a conference about what Agile really was. I got a lot of amorphous answers, so I kept pushing. It finally came down, always, to a simple goal: we want the software faster.

So, your challenge will be explaining to managers and executives how there is such a thing as enough testing and such a thing as not enough testing. You also have to explain that tools are not magic, but involve hard work, skills, and expertise.

You will have an ever-increasing number of mobile testing resources available, in terms of testing service providers, tools, cloud testing, crowdsourcing, and so forth. There will be new and expanded ways to involve the end user in the testing process.

However the process changes, these tools, these resources, while potentially helpful, will not replace smart testers making smart testing decisions.

> The whole history of software life cycles is a long one, but a short version goes like this. In the early days of software engineering, there were two basic life cycles. One was waterfall, where you carefully specify requirements, then design the system to meet those requirements, then build that system, then test it. Basically, it's the software version of how bridges and buildings are created. The other life cycle—or really anti-life cycle—was code-and-fix. You just write whatever you think will work, throw it against the wall, and see if it sticks.
>
> In the 1990s, the Rational Unified Process (RUP) and Rapid Application Development (RAD) emerged, which basically broke the waterfall into a series of overlapping mini-waterfalls, each focused on building a specific subset of features. That gave way to Agile life cycles such as Scrum and XP, starting in the late 1990s. In the 2000s and now 2010s, we've seen Lean, Kanban, and now DevOps grow out of Agile.

As long as we continue to believe, as an industry, that getting the process right will save us, that the process is the key to speedy delivery, that the process is the key to quality, we will continue to see life cycle churn. The same pattern will repeat. Last year's newest and greatest process ideas will be revealed as not actually being magic bullets, only to be replaced by the next great idea in the software engineering process.

Eventually someone will realize that improving the software engineering process is just part of the puzzle. Clearly, having an organized, carefully designed life cycle will result in better software. However, even a perfect life cycle won't solve all of the challenges of software engineering.

5.3 Test your knowledge

Let's try one or more sample exam questions related to the material we've just covered. The answers are found in Appendix C.

Question 5 Learning objective: MOB-5.3.1 (K2) Explain how life cycle models are likely to change and how this will affect testing

In the future, mobile software development life cycles will:

    A.   return entirely to waterfall variations;

    B.   remain primarily Agile;

    C.   require quality activities throughout the process;

    D.   involve testers only at the end.

4 ANTICIPATING THE FUTURE

The learning objective for Chapter 5, Section 4, is:

MOB-5.4.1   (K1) Recall the ways in which testers will need to adapt.

So, as I've said, you should expect processes to continue to churn. New tools will bring change. Testing practices will continue to change, especially in the dynamic world of mobile development, as well as for other emerging technologies such as robotics, the Internet of Things, artificial intelligence, virtual reality, self-driving cars, and 3D printing. However, remember that the best practices that have been established in testing for years and years abide, although they are often ignored.

For example, a very large number of people get paid to be professional testers. Less than half of those testers, however, could sit down and properly apply equivalence partitioning to design a test for an input screen. Equivalence partitioning is the most basic fundamental of black-box test design techniques.[5]

This matters because, when people actually do know how to apply fundamental black-box test design techniques, it makes a big difference. I have had clients tell me that, by applying equivalence partitioning to their testing, they increased their efficiency by over 50 percent.

---

[5] There are no industry studies to back up this statistic, but I have spent the last 20 years delivering training as well as other consulting and expert services to clients around the world and I've seen well over half of testers unable to apply the equivalent partitioning technique prior to my training them how to do it.

So, learn to apply these proven best practices. Some people believe that mobile technologies change everything, but this is the hype cycle again. Mobile technologies don't change everything. Proven testing best practices still work, but the way you apply those proven best practices does change.

Over the previous chapters of this book, I've talked quite a bit about investments in tests, test data, tools, test automation, test environments, and the like. These are important decisions, and should be made in a thoughtful way. So, try to plan out two years, three years, or further, depending on the size of the investment that you're going to make in your test environments.

Another theme in this book has been the fierce competition in the mobile devices and apps markets. On the device side, we see a relentless attempt by the mobile device makers to avoid commoditization. I don't have access to device-maker executive strategies, but I have to believe that many of them understand what happens when you get commoditized because they have been in or continue to be in commoditized markets, or have just paid attention to what happened with PCs. Whatever the specific motivations are, the pace of innovation and new feature deployment on the device-side will likely remain rapid.

The competition is a little different on the app side. On the device side you have a few dozen device manufacturers, and it can only grow so much. There are natural limits to the growth in device manufacturers. There are some pretty significant barriers to entry, at least so long as the components resist commoditization and cannot be bought as easily as, say, the components that make up a PC or laptop.

In the case of apps, there are around six million apps on the market already. Not every app is made by a different company, so there aren't four million app-making companies, but there are a tremendously large number of companies creating mobile apps. The barriers to entry are entirely non-existent. Anybody can download a mobile OS software development toolkit (SDK), start building apps, and put them in an app store. So, the competition there is all about differentiation in an already-commoditized mobile app market. The competition is likely to continue to be as brutal as a Dickensian orphanage. That kind of competition is no fun from the inside, but it tends to take Schumpeter's economic concept of creative destruction to new highs, and it will drive a lot of change.[6]

This means that you must be ready to learn a lot of new stuff in a short period of time. You'll need to take some chances and take some smart risks. If you make mistakes—and you probably will—be sure to learn from them. When you take risks, take calculated ones where you can find out whether the risk is going to pay off quickly.

For example, if you take risks with test automation, do it in such a way that you'll discover quickly whether your automation approach will actually work and have a positive return on investment. Remember the cautionary tales I told you about companies finding they had a negative return on investment after years of working on their test automation. You don't want to go through that experience.

---

[6] You can find a good explanation of creative destruction, or "Schumpeter's gale," here: www.econlib.org/library/Enc/CreativeDestruction.html

If you're going to try something that fails, you want to be able to recognize it as a failure quickly. This is what's sometimes referred to as failing fast. Unfortunately, sometimes this fail-fast mantra gets used to justify the software version of throwing half-cooked spaghetti at the wall—an excuse for trying wild ideas with little chance of success. Remember, it's not true that it doesn't matter how many times you fail. Frequent failure is not efficient. Ready, fire, aim is how you shoot a machine gun, which is fine if you don't care about the fact that you're paying a dollar a round. You get more efficient results with a scoped rifle, where a single well-aimed shot hits the bullseye and where failure to hit the bullseye results in adjustments to the scope, producing a better-placed shot next time.

So, if you miss the bullseye, adjust your scope and try again. How do you adjust your scope? Part of it is assessment of what went wrong. Part of it is also learning from other people's successes and failures. Do industry research. Study industry trends. Read books on testing, test automation, mobile technologies, and so forth. Learn to write scripts and apps. Learn to program. Learn how to use new testing tools. Read technical publications that discuss emerging technologies, new phones and mobile devices, and so forth.

When things are really moving fast, it really helps to be a geek. By geek, I mean that this is your thing. A geek is someone who gets really excited about whatever it is that geeks them out.

For example, I have a few clients in the video gaming space. I've met a lot of game testers. Each of them is a hardcore gamer. It is their thing. They play games at work as part of testing them. They go home from work and play games. They read about games in trade journals and online.

Anytime you're dealing with something that's really dynamic and fast moving, it helps if you find the whole subject fascinating and you love immersing yourself in it. If it's boring to you, and it's just a job, it will be harder to keep up.

A final word of advice, to expand on something I said earlier. Resist the mindset or slogan of "this changes everything." It's just part of the hype cycle, and I see this with some of my clients.

In the early days of Agile, I would hear people say, "Agile changes everything and no traditional testing best practices apply in Agile." What's happened over the last 20 years is that people have figured out how to apply traditional testing best practices to Agile, and now people realize that about 90 percent of traditional testing best practices can be and should be incorporated into Agile.

It's the same thing with mobile. I hear people say, "Mobile changes everything about testing." Well, it changes some things, for sure, and I've discussed some of them in this book.

However, things that come along and change everything, literally everything, these things are really rare. Learning how to extract mechanical energy by burning coal at the start of the Industrial Revolution, yes, that literally changed everything. Learning how to fix nitrogen by making ammonia, thus freeing ourselves from a dependency on bird guano as a source of nitrogen, yes, that literally changed everything. Learning how to split the atom, yes, that was a game changer for sure.

However, if we are talking about computer-related advances that might change everything, something that qualifies for that breathless phrase is the concept of convergence, the loading of human consciousness into a computer. Yes, that really will change everything, because that's going to be the end of human mortality and that is pretty discontinuous.

Mobile changing everything? Yeah, sure, right, just like Agile changed everything. Whenever I hear people saying "X changes everything," my immediate thought is that we have somebody pushing some hype. And, being the cynical guy I am, I ask myself, "How are they making money off the hype?"

So, soldier on, and apply and adapt existing testing best practices to mobile testing whilst learning how to apply the new best practices that are emerging for testing mobile apps. To paraphrase the aphorism, have the serenity to accept the things that remain the same, the courage to master the things that do change, and the wisdom to know the difference.

5.4 Test your knowledge

Let's try one or more sample exam questions related to the material we've just covered. The answers are found in Appendix C.

> Question 6 Learning objective: MOB-5.4.1 (K1) Recall the ways in which testers will need to adapt

As a mobile tester, you will need to:

    A. Be ready to learn new skills as technologies evolve.
    B. Move into development since testing is fading out as a career.
    C. Focus on non-functional testing.
    D. Focus on mastering existing tools.

In this final, brief chapter we addressed the rapid growth you must expect in the mobile app testing world. We saw that flexibility and readiness for change are key. In addition, successful mobile app testers plan for the future, and try to see around corners as the future comes towards them.

6   APPENDICES

APPENDIX A: REFERENCES AND RESOURCES

The ASTQB Certified Mobile Tester syllabus provides some references and resources that may be useful to you.

BIBLIOGRAPHY

The Certified Mobile Tester syllabus references the following books. They can be useful resources for you as you learn more about mobile testing:

- Rex Black (2009) *Managing the Testing Process, 3e*. Hoboken, NJ: John Wiley & Sons.

- Maximiliano Firtman (2013) *Programming the Mobile Web*. Sebastopol, CA: O'Reilly Media.

- Erik van Veenendaal (2006) *Practical Risk-based Testing*. s-Hertogenbosch: UTN Publishers.

- James Whittaker, et al. (2012) *How Google Tests Software*. Boston, MA: Addison-Wesley Professional.

The Certified Mobile Tester syllabus also references the following documents:

- ISTQB® Advanced Test Analyst Syllabus 2018

- ISTQB® Certified Tester Foundation Level Overview

- ISTQB® Certified Tester Foundation Level Syllabus 2018

- ISTQB® Standard Glossary

The Certified Mobile Tester syllabus also references the following resources.

- InfoQ, www.infoq.com/news/2014/10/world-quality-report

- Greg Paskal, www.gregpaskal.com

- Open Device Lab, www.opendevicelab.com

- OWASP, www.owasp.org/index.php/Projects/OWASP_Mobile_Security_Project_-_Top_Ten_Mobile_Risks

- Jakob Nielsen, "Why you only need to test with 5 testers," www.useit.com

APPENDIX B: EXERCISE SOLUTIONS

The following sections give general guidance for exercise solutions.

3.2 Functional test design

In looking at your own solution, ask yourself some questions.

First, did you cover both valid and invalid inputs? Most people who have been testers for a while are good at testing with invalids, and in fact sometimes over-emphasize those tests and don't cover important valid conditions.

Second, which tests would you run first? Some people like to start with the various invalid inputs, forcing lots of error conditions. That approach is fine for a stable application, but for less-stable applications it's usually better to run some basic valid tests first.

3.3 Performance testing

While the specifics will vary with your chosen app, your performance testing approach should address the following areas:

- The types of users and how they interact with the software.
- The performance goals you have on the client-side and the server-side.
- How frequently you want to do performance testing.
- The types of devices you'll use.
- The role simulators will play.

Keep in mind that mobile app users will compare your app's performance to that of other mobile apps and will also be very sensitive to any negative changes in your app's performance after an upgrade.

As an example, assume you are testing an app that allows users to manage their travel, with data stored both locally and on the internet. Consider testing the response time the app requires to sync with the server after the user has created a new trip.

The tests will analyze the changes in response time occurring as a result of different forms of connectivity: Wi-Fi, 3G, offline, etc. There are many different types of users that are expected to be using the app in these situations:

- The first-time user is someone who has just downloaded the app and hopes to use it to plan an upcoming trip. They would hope the app is simple and easy enough to use that they could quickly plan the upcoming trip with no hassle.
- The casual user is someone who uses the app once or twice a year to plan a trip (most likely a vacation). They would want either reminders about how to use the app or a simple enough experience that can be remembered.

- The heavy user most likely frequently plans last minute business trips and is constantly traveling. They would need the app to be consistently reliable and allow changes without difficulty.

- The frustrated or angry user such as one who just had a flight changed or cancelled needs the app to work at that moment so they can find a new flight without getting angrier.

- The impatient user wants the app to work quickly.

- The intimidated user is not confident in their abilities to use the app and needs guidance through the app.

- The confused user needs careful explanations and an easy-to-understand interface in order to continue using the app.

All personas will hope for a fast performing app that will allow the user to accomplish any goal in a timely manner with little or no hassle.

The performance goal for the server-side is fast turnaround of a data transfer, so that the trip syncs quickly and the user can continue to use the app. The specific meaning of fast enough turnaround can be determined by talking to stakeholders and benchmarking other mobile apps. The client-side should indicate what is occurring while the trip is being synced (for example, through a progress bar) to avoid as much user-frustration as possible, and it should notify the user if the sync fails due to connectivity issues.

This performance testing should be required at least once per update, but preferably it would be run very frequently to quickly correct any problems that may arise from server issues.

It is important to test this on a range of different devices; it could be tested on a range of brands. Simulators can be used, but the tester must be wary and ensure that they work correctly in order to gather information from them.

3.3 Usability testing

While here again the specifics will vary with your chosen app, your usability approach should address the following areas:

- The types of users and how they interact with the software (i.e. the user personas). The easiest way to do this is to build on your performance tests from the previous exercise.

- Next, for each user persona, discuss how you intend to test user expectations. What should you look for in terms of look and feel, including color schemes, fonts, images, and themes? How will you gauge the attractiveness of the user interface? How will you evaluate learnability and understandability, again considering each user persona?

- You should consider any built-in devices and supported peripherals, and how you will evaluate the usability implications there. Remember that the usability of these devices and peripherals will affect the users' perceptions of the usability of your app, fairly or unfairly.

- You should also be sure to evaluate usability across all the tasks the users will carry out, again considering the different personas. It's possible that one persona would find usability during one task perfectly acceptable, while another persona could be completely infuriated by the usability attributes of that same task. Further, one persona could be happy with one task's usability and infuriated by another task's usability.

During the hands-on portion of the exercise, you should have selected three of these tasks to carry out. I suggested a time box of five minutes, but of course you could have spent longer. During that time, you should have measured the following:

- The number of times you managed to complete each task.

- The time required to perform each task, each time you performed it.

- The number of mistakes made in each task, each time your performed it.

- The number of distinct actions (swipes, inputs, etc.) necessary to do each task, each time your performed it.

Assuming you were able to do each of the three tasks multiple times, you can measure learnability by comparing the metrics from each iteration. If the time required to perform each task, the number of mistakes made, and the number of distinct actions all went down, and went down quickly, that would indicate a good level of learnability.

As an example, let's continue on with the previous hypothetical travel management app. We can use the same personas as the previous exercise covering performance testing. The user expectations for the application are mainly focused on the functional side of the application.

The application will be expected to accomplish what needs to be done in a timely manner, whilst allowing the user to understand what is happening in the app. It should have the smallest learning curve possible and allow effective navigation between screens. It also needs to allow customization, but it should function well enough in its initial, unmodified form that the user isn't required to change the settings to effectively use the app.

The largest concern the app should have with devices is cooperation with the operating system's keyboard, because that is what the user will be using to communicate with the app. It can support other functions, such as voice typing, but the most essential is support for the keyboard. I would test the app with Bluetooth keyboards as well.

There are hundreds of tasks that can be used to test the usability of a travel management app, but consider the following possibilities:

- Add a family travel contact.

- Change notification settings to never alert.

- Change the app's automatic data refresh to once per day.

- Add an upcoming trip.

- View past trips.

4.1 Tools

Depending on your app, the tests you need to automate, and whether you want to automate on the device itself, on the server, or on both, will vary. Your solution should cover the following types of tests:

- **Functionality:** For example, you might want to build tests that cover all new functionality, or you might want to focus on regression testing of key functionality over time.
- **Performance and reliability:** For these types of tests, you may need load generation on the server-side, which is fairly traditional, or you may be focused entirely on the device-side, which is very different.
- **Security:** For some apps, security may not be a worry at all, but for others it could be quite an issue. Security tools can focus on the servers on the network as a whole, or on the application itself.
- **Portability:** For many mobile apps, portability is a huge concern. Automation of portability tests can be a real challenge, though, so you will need to proceed with caution.

In the second part of the exercise, I told you to search the web to identify tools for each type, with the goal of identifying at least one commercial and one open-source option for each. Now, I should confess, these instructions were actually in conflict somewhat with what I told you in the book, where I said you should only start looking at tools once you had fully evaluated your requirements. The rationale behind this step of the exercise, though, was not to actually start tool selection, but rather to bring home the point that there are many, many tool options in many cases.

4.2 Environments and protocols

As before, your solution will vary depending on your chosen app. That said, test environments and protocols are a huge consideration for mobile apps, so you should have carefully considered the following points including:

- **Data handling and protocols:** Many apps both send and receive data frequently, and are used in areas with fluctuating connectivity. In such a case, one data issue that needs to be considered is specifically what happens to the data when it is transmitting and the connection goes down. The upload or download of data needs to be able to quickly resume once a connection is reestablished so the user does not have to manually resume the download or wait a long time for the data to start over from the beginning. Further, the data transfer should resume where it left off, not discard the data already sent and start over, which is both time consuming and, depending on the user's data plan, potentially costly. Additionally, if the data being transferred contains sensitive information, the app has to keep the data safe at all times.
- **Device capabilities and features:** In many cases, apps need to be available and work well on many different types of devices. If so, your app needs to work with a wide variety of different components. Various types of network capabilities,

as well as possibly different Bluetooth standards, will all need to cooperate. If yours is a text-heavy app, you'll need to address soft keyboards and Bluetooth keyboards. Many screen resolutions, as well as sizes, should be tested to accommodate a wide range of devices and different manufacturers should be tested as well.

- **Real-world stuff:** The real world is nothing like the pristine testing conditions that one may find in a testing lab. It is important to test inclement events such as disconnections, low battery modes, shutdowns, incoming calls, and the like, so that the app can be fully prepared for what may happen in the real world. The tester should test as many such incidents as possible to ensure the best possible performance for the app. Your app could suffer from power failures, incoming or outgoing call interruptions and network drops or bottlenecks, to name just a few issues. All of these, and more, should be tested in order to avoid problems with customers regarding this real-world stuff.

- **Connectivity:** If people use your app for real-time problem solving, then, after reliability, connectivity is arguably the most important aspect. People may depend on your app to give them status updates and to allow them to solve problems quickly, so the app must be tested on as many different networks as possible. Connectivity will be a constantly changing factor for the app; issues could include rapidly fluctuating network capabilities or semi-frequent drops in service, depending on the users' location, and both the server and the client should be able to cope with them effectively and efficiently.

- **Memory:** Most users use other apps in parallel with your app. It is really inconvenient if the app has to restart every time the user opens it because the memory capabilities of the phone cannot handle the load on the RAM. The app should be able to run in the background with low memory usage so it is ready for the user whenever they decide to open it. Additionally, users will expect it to take up only a small space in the device's storage, and the app will need to be small enough to be able to be downloaded off a wireless signal (some carriers limit the size of app downloads over cellular data).

This may not be a primary concern, but the app should work well when running off expanded or external storage like a micro SD card or flash drive, assuming that is possible. If the app itself can't reside on such expanded or external storage, but it can store data on such storage, that should be tested.

4.4 Real devices, simulators, emulators, and the cloud

Adequate testing for your app may require testing to be done under a wide variety of connections in order to ensure that the app will work, no matter how it is connected. To best test this, real devices with actual connections need to be used, and they need to be mobile as well. Just sitting in a test lab, bathed in strong cellular and Wi-Fi signals, is not representative of your users' realities, so don't do all your testing like that.

You may also have decided to include open device labs and remote device labs in your solution. This can help expand device coverage, but may not do much to address fluctuations in connectivity resulting from moving through different settings. However, maybe the main point is to expand device coverage and you're comfortable with your ability to adequately address connectivity issues with your own devices, or in some other way.

Crowdsourcing is one way to test the connectivity of your app across a wide number of devices and connectivity settings. Crowdsourcing companies can be hired. Alternatively, you could assemble a DIY crowdsourcing program in the form of a beta test, but you'll need to figure out how to attract adequate testers. Beta testers could be incentivized to test the app by offering rewards such as a free month of a premium subscription or the removal of ads. This way, the actual users of the app can offer feedback while testing. However, keep in mind that such users often are not professional testers, and the quality of the testing done, the results reporting, and the details of the bugs found can be lower than what you might expect from professional testers.

Cloud-based network simulators might also be used to provide the necessary network configurations to test the app. The tester should be careful using this option, since cloud services are not always reliable. Some of my clients have reported such problems. Some results from the cloud simulations should be compared to tests with real devices to verify their integrity.

4.6 Test automation

As always, your specific solution will vary, depending on your app. Suppose you are testing a travel management app. On such an app, the main use cases would involve adding or editing trips, adding travel documents and travel contacts and changing settings. Here are the keywords:

    A. Add_Trip
    B. Add_Plan (if necessary, this could be broken up into finer-grained keywords such as Add_Plan_Flight, Add_Plan_Lodging, and so forth)
    C. Add_Document (this could also be broken into finer-grained keywords such as Add_Document_Passport, Add_Document_DriverLicense, and so forth)
    D. Add_Contact
    E. Sign_Out
    F. Add_to_Calendar

Table A.1 shows the keyword-driven table. Note that the symbolic or logical values shown in the columns in the table would need to be replaced with actual values as part of implementing the tests.

5.2 Build for change

Assuming your app is a long-term solution for its users, rather than just a passing fad, then it needs to be treated as such. When looking for tools and vendors or partners, the main quality the tester should look for in these tools and companies (after accuracy) should be reliability. Of course, the financial realities of the organization will determine whether you can choose a more expensive but better option, or if you must settle for something less than ideal. If you do have to settle, be extra careful, but the old adage

Table A.1 Keyword-driven tests for the travel app

Keyword	Data1	Data2	Data3	Data4	Expected result
Add_Trip	Destination	Start date	End date		Trip added
Add_Trip	Start date	End date	Trip name		Trip added
Add_Trip	Destination	Start date	End date	Trip name	Trip added
Add_Trip	Destination	Start date	Trip name		Error message
Add_Trip	End date				Error message
Add_Plan	Flight	Flight #	Departure date	Arrival date	Flight added
Add_Plan	Lodging	Departure date	Address	Arrival date	Lodging added
Add_Plan	Flight	Departure date			Error message
Add_Plan	Departure date				Error message
Add_Document	Correct PIN	Passport	Passport number		Passport added
Add_Document	Correct PIN	Driver license	Number		Driver license added
Add_Document	Correct PIN	Passport			Error message
Add_Document	Correct PIN	Driver license			Error message
Add_Document	Incorrect PIN				Error message
Add_Contact	Correct PIN	Emergency contact	Name		Contact added
Add_Contact	Correct PIN	Emergency contact			Error message
Add_Contact	Incorrect PIN				Error message
Sign_Out	Ok				User signed out
Sign_Out	Cancel				User not signed out
Add_to_Calendar	Add				Trip is added to Google Calendar
Add_to_Calendar	Cancel				Trip is not added to Google Calendar

155

"penny wise and pound foolish" is an adage for a reason. Your app needs testers that will continue to test as the mobile market, and the functionality of the app, expands and that usually means the use of established stable testing companies. Open-source tools can be used, certainly. Make sure the communities behind these tools are likely to stick with the tool and maintain it. Commercial tool companies may seem more reliable, but you never know, companies do come and go. As technology and the market change, the tools used to test your app have to remain up to date to avoid any issues that may arise because the app was tested inadequately.

Test design and documentation should be understandable and adequately test the app, but it should also avoid being so specific that it has to be rewritten every time a small part of the app is changed. The testing should really only require minor changes as long as the app does the same fundamental processes and doesn't undergo a complete overhaul.

Additionally, the tester in charge of automation should have at least five years of automation experience and mobile experience as well. This helps to ensure that the automation decisions made do not have the effect of painting the test automation effort into a corner. When that does happen, all the investments made in automation must be scrapped and a new start made. This is a very painful decision that often is not made until long after it should have been. It's best to avoid this situation rather than to have to deal with the professional and business ramifications of it.

APPENDIX C: SAMPLE EXAM QUESTION ANSWERS AND EXPLANATIONS

CHAPTER 1

1.1 Test your knowledge

Question 1 Correct answer: **D**

A. Incorrect. Some apps are more portable than others, but most apps are not completely portable.
B. Incorrect. While some apps run within browsers on mobile devices, some are native.
C. Incorrect. While some apps run within browsers on mobile devices, some are native.
D. Correct. The growth rate of mobile apps is accelerating over time.

Question 2 Correct answer: **C**

A. Incorrect. A describes a hybrid application.
B. Incorrect. B describes a mobile web application.
C. Correct. C gives the definition of a native mobile application.
D. Incorrect. D gives the definition of a native device.

1.2 Test your knowledge

Question 3 Correct answer: **A**

A. Correct. There are usually many options for common applications.
B. Incorrect. Most apps are easy to replace, with many options available.
C. Incorrect. The specific problem mentioned is usability, not performance.
D. Incorrect. While this statement is true, it's quite likely that the user will have abandoned the app by then.

1.3 Test your knowledge

Question 4 Correct answer: **B**

 A. Incorrect. The cost of obtaining complete mobile app development environments is close to zero, though the cost of complete testing environments can be very high.

 B. Correct. While the cost of obtaining complete mobile app development environments is close to zero, the cost of complete testing environments can be very high.

 C. Incorrect. Frequent releases are a major challenge for testers, and even the use of Agile methods doesn't entirely resolve the problem.

 D. Incorrect. For many mobile apps, portability testing is a significant challenge.

Question 5 Correct answer: **A**

 A. Correct. With mobile websites, the app is hosted on the server but allows mobile access across multiple compatible devices via their browsers.

 B. Incorrect. Native apps include code specifically written for host devices.

 C. Incorrect. While hybrid apps are designed to be portable, they do have code running on the target devices.

 D. Incorrect. Mobile websites have the app hosted on the server, accessed via various devices via their browsers.

1.4 Test your knowledge

Question 6 Correct answer: **D**

 A. Incorrect. The test design techniques covered in the ISTQB® Certified Tester Foundation and Test Analyst syllabi 2018 are useful in mobile testing, but there are other techniques as well that have been developed for testing mobile apps.

 B. Incorrect. The test design techniques covered in the ISTQB® Certified Tester Foundation and Test Analyst syllabi 2018 are useful in mobile testing, though there are other techniques as well that have been developed for testing mobile apps.

 C. Incorrect. The ASTQB Mobile Tester syllabus describes a number of best practices in mobile testing that are evolving. Exploratory testing is but one technique that should be used

 D. Correct. The test design techniques covered in the ISTQB® Certified Tester Foundation and Test Analyst syllabi 2018 are useful in mobile testing, but there are other techniques as well that have been developed for testing mobile apps.

1.5 Test Your Knowledge

Question 7 Correct answer: **D**

A. Incorrect. Option A describes just one of the ways to reduce the number of tests with equivalence partitioning.
B. Incorrect. Option B describes the use of boundary value analysis.
C. Incorrect. All the techniques described in the Foundation and Test Analyst syllabi can be applied to mobile testing.
D. Correct. Many test situations, including the selection of test devices, can be handled through equivalence partitioning.

1.6 Test your knowledge

Question 8 Correct answer: **D**

A. Incorrect. Agile life cycles are used for mobile app development, but the use of Agile methods increases the regression risk that must be managed through testing.
B. Incorrect. In mobile app development, documentation of tests is usually lightweight due to time constraints.
C. Incorrect. Spiral models are actually a good way to identify and mitigate technical risk during new feature development.
D. Correct. Incremental and iterative life cycles can be used to quickly release new features as the user base evolves. However, it's important that adequate testing is performed against these quick releases to avoid distributing low-quality software to users.

CHAPTER 2

2.1 Test your knowledge

Question 1 Correct answer: **C**

A. Incorrect. While use cases do help developers build an application that meets the users' needs, that does not address why use cases help you test.
B. Incorrect. Option B describes how decision tables are used for testing.
C. Correct. Use cases state how actors, often users, accomplish goals using an application.
D. Incorrect. While use cases can be used to create operational profiles for performance and reliability testing, it's not the reason why use cases are helpful but simply one way to use them.

2.2 Test your knowledge

Question 2 Correct answer: **D**

    A. Incorrect. Since the test object is a new application, there are no production metrics.

    B. Incorrect. Option B might be a good step, as a first step you should identify some initial risks to seed the process.

    C. Incorrect. The risks must be identified before they can be assessed.

    D. Correct. Whilst you'll need the help of other project participants to complete the risk identification, having examples is useful as part of the meeting invitation.

2.3 Test your knowledge

Question 3 Correct answer: **A**

    A. Correct. In addition to connectivity, requirements, functions, and devices are mentioned.

    B. Incorrect. There's no discussion of what could go wrong (i.e. risks), but connectivity, requirements, functions, and devices are mentioned.

    C. Incorrect. There's no discussion of how to address structural coverage, but connectivity, requirements, functions, and devices are mentioned.

    D. Incorrect. Connectivity, requirements, functions, and devices are mentioned.

Question 4 Correct answer: **A**

    A. Correct. Option A is the Glossary definition.

    B. Incorrect. Option B is the definition of an operational environment.

    C. Incorrect. Option C is the definition of operational testing.

    D. Incorrect. Option D is part of the definition for random testing.

2.4 Test your knowledge

Question 5 Correct answer: **A**

    A. Correct. As per the ASTQB Certified Mobile Tester syllabus, scheduling (i.e. prioritization) of tests is addressed in the test approach.

    B. Incorrect. Evaluation of pass/fail status of a test is determined by the test oracle.

    C. Incorrect. Staff turnover is a project risk, not a quality risk.

    D. Incorrect. The need to do accessibility testing is determined by target audience and by regulations.

2.5 Test your knowledge

Question 6 Correct answer: **C**

    A. Incorrect. Option A describes a test case, not a test condition.
    B. Incorrect. Option B describes a test condition related to the functional capabilities of the app.
    C. Correct. Locating a petrol station involves testing geolocation as well as the app functions.
    D. Incorrect. Option C describes a test condition related to non-functional behavior, specifically recovery (which is part of reliability).

2.6 Test your knowledge

Question 7 Correct answer: **C**

    A. Incorrect. There are multiple ways to automate mobile tests.
    B. Incorrect. If anything, the rapid change of the apps makes mobile apps more subject to regression.
    C. Correct. Device and device software changes can affect mobile apps.
    D. Incorrect. Simulators do not capture all possible behaviors and uses, especially physical ones.

CHAPTER 3

3.1 Test your knowledge

Question 1 Correct answer: **B**

    A. Incorrect. Option A is the definition of a wild pointer.
    B. Correct. Option B is the definition of geolocation per the ASTQB Mobile Tester Glossary.
    C. Incorrect. Option C is the definition of a pointer.
    D. Incorrect. Option D is the definition of a geotag.

3.2 Test your knowledge

Question 2 Correct answer: **C**

To cover the equivalent partitions, you should test one non-supported card, and you should test one valid and one invalid card number for each of the three supported card types. Therefore, the answer is C.

Question 3 Correct answers: **B and E**

    A.   Incorrect. Response time is part of performance testing.

    B.   Correct. Suitability is one attribute of correctness.

    C.   Incorrect. The syllabus classifies security as part of functional testing, but not correctness.

    D.   Incorrect. The syllabus classifies interoperability as part of functional testing, but not correctness.

    E.   Correct. Accuracy is one attribute of correctness.

Question 4 Correct answer: **D**

    A.   Incorrect. The user has possession of the device, so lost devices is not an explanation here.

    B.   Incorrect. Donation of a device is not an explanation here because the information captured is of the current, not the former, user.

    C.   Incorrect. The browser, not some other downloaded app, is what's being used in this scenario.

    D.   Correct. Ease of attacking mobile devices is a vulnerability associated with using a public Wi-Fi hotspot.

Question 5 Correct answer: **B**

    A.   Incorrect. Unless the UI has dramatically changed over the last few days, there is no reason for a frequent user to be startled by your application's user interface.

    B.   Correct. Since the first-time user hasn't seen the user interface before, it could startle them.

    C.   Incorrect. A technically knowledgeable user is the least likely type of user to be confused or startled.

    D.   Incorrect. Option D is a possible answer, but an impatient user might also be quite knowledgeable about the application.

Question 6 Correct answer: **A**

    A.   Correct. Since each device supported must report exactly the same position, device differences are a concern.

    B.   Incorrect. Security is not a primary concern, as you might not care if the active shooter knows that you are locating him, as long as you can locate him.

    C.   Incorrect. There is no mention of supported peripherals in this scenario.

    D.   Incorrect. There is no mention that over-the-air upgrades are supported for this app.

Question 7 Correct answer: **D**

A. Incorrect. One objective of the technique is to use brainstorming to transcend requirements, rather than being dependent on the requirements.
B. Incorrect. TestStorming is a form of brainstorming.
C. Incorrect. TestStorming tests can be functional or non-functional when created by this technique.
D. Correct. Like all forms of brainstorming, the idea of TestStorming is an open-ended process to harness the collective wisdom of the participants.

3.3 Test your knowledge

Question 8 Correct answer: **A**

A. Correct. Since the simulator runs on a PC, it will have more CPU and memory available to it, especially given the parallel applications running on the mobile device hosts, differences in CPU and memory utilization between the PC and the mobile devices can be significant.
B. Incorrect. It would be easy to generate streams of images and weather data for the application.
C. Incorrect. Nothing in the outlined scenario suggests that no simulator would be available.
D. Incorrect. While lack of performance testing skills can be an issue for any performance test, it is not an issue specific to simulators.

Question 9 Correct answer: **D**

A. Incorrect. The processing of data in real time requires predictable, regular response time but a slow launch is not particularly relevant.
B. Incorrect. The processing of data gathered from network-accessible devices in real time requires regular response time but the user interface response can be slower.
C. Incorrect. The processing of data in real time requires predictable, regular response time, which is not a function of application usability.
D. Correct. The processing of data in real time requires predictable, regular response time.

Question 10 Correct answer: **B**

A. Incorrect. Only one task, location of a criminal, is listed in the scenario.
B. Correct. Since seconds count in these types of situations, time to complete a task is critical.
C. Incorrect. Resource usage is a metric for performance, reliability, and portability.
D. Incorrect. Simplicity is an important attribute but it is not a measurement.

Question 11 Correct answer: **C**

    A. Incorrect. Resource utilization is a general reliability measurement for any application.

    B. Incorrect. Mean time between failure is a general reliability measurement for any application.

    C. Correct. Excessive power consumption (for example, from overly frequent querying of devices) could result in quick failure of the application when the battery is exhausted.

    D. Incorrect. Loss of connectivity is a general reliability measurement for any application that must send and receive data from other devices.

CHAPTER 4

4.1 Test your knowledge

Question 1 Correct answer: **B**

    A. Incorrect. Browser independence could also apply to PC test tools.

    B. Correct. Simulating changing location is mobile-specific because mobile devices are, well, mobile.

    C. Incorrect. Working with various network speeds could apply to any test of a networked application.

    D. Incorrect. Simulating loss of network connectivity could apply to any test of a networked application.

Question 2 Correct answer: **D**

    A. Incorrect. Web server performance test tools are not necessary for all mobile testing because not all mobile apps will have a web-based subsystem.

    B. Incorrect. Android platform simulators are not generic tools.

    C. Incorrect. Telecom mobile protocol simulators are not generic tools.

    D. Correct. Bug-tracking tools are generic tools which are useful for any mobile testing projects, since any testing effort will result in finding bugs unless you have perfect developers.

4.2 Test your knowledge

Question 3 Correct answer: **B**

    A. Incorrect. Web server data are common to any internet system.

    B. Correct. An accelerometer is a sensor on a mobile device.

C. Incorrect. A cloud-testing service is used for testing internet servers as well.

D. Incorrect. A Bluetooth keyboard can be used with any Bluetooth-enabled device.

Question 4 Correct answer: **D**

A. Incorrect. Simulators are not a good way to test connection speed variations.

B. Incorrect. You want to keep the new features secret and crowdsourcing would involve exposing those features to strangers.

C. Incorrect. Used and refurbished devices are often underpowered compared to recent devices and likely to exhibit lots of false positives in terms of performance, connection speed, and reliability.

D. Correct. You'll need to generate load for testing reliability and performance on the server-side.

4.3 Test your knowledge

Question 5 Correct answer: **A**

A. Correct. Major plug-ins often have problems with specific browsers and devices.

B. Incorrect. Simulators are most typically used for native app testing.

C. Incorrect. Both browser-based and native apps typically have server components, so server-side performance degradation is not more likely in a browser-based application.

D. Incorrect. Lack of tool support is a challenge but it is not a bug in an application.

Question 6 Correct answer: **A**

A. Correct. Option A is the Glossary definition of an emulator.

B. Incorrect. Option B is the Glossary definition of a simulator.

C. Incorrect. Option C is the Glossary definition of a native device.

D. Incorrect. Option D is the Glossary definition of geolocation.

4.4 Test your knowledge

Question 7 Correct answer: **B**

A. Incorrect. Realism of test results is a reason why real devices must be used to some extent.

B. Correct. Simulators are often available for free.

C. Incorrect. Leakage of trade secrets is an example of a potential problem with cloud-testing services.

D. Incorrect. Browsers are widely available on mobile and PC platforms.

Question 8 Correct answer: **A**

A. Correct. Developers will use the Android simulators during development and unit testing, cloud-hosted devices can be used for functionality and compatibility testing during system tests, and crowdsourcing across a diverse set of devices in the real world will be a good beta test. The iOS simulator will not be used, since we are only supporting Android at this time.

B. Incorrect. Developers will use the Android simulators during development and unit testing, but the iOS simulator is not useful as we're only supporting Android initially. Cloud-hosted devices can be used for functionality and compatibility testing during system test. Crowdsourcing across a diverse set of devices in the real world will be a good beta test.

C. Incorrect. Developers will use the Android simulators—but not iOS—simulators during development and unit testing, as during that time the app is not ready for real-world use. Cloud-hosted devices can be used for functionality and compatibility testing during system testing, prior to beta testing. Beta testing would typically not involve cloud-hosted devices.

D. Incorrect. Developers will use the Android simulators, not iOS simulators, during development and unit testing, due to the initial support goal of Android only. Otherwise, this is correct in that cloud-hosted devices can be used for functionality and compatibility testing during system testing, and crowdsourcing across a diverse set of devices in the real world will be a good beta test.

Question 9 Correct answer: **D**

A. Incorrect. The simulator vendor may not even know about all discrepancies that exist.

B. Incorrect. There is no guarantee that a commercial simulator will be more realistic than an open-source simulator.

C. Incorrect. Generating large volumes of user input is an issue for load testing, not functional testing.

D. Correct. Compare real device behavior to simulator behavior, and, if the simulator gives the same results, it's reliable.

4.5 Test your knowledge

Question 10 Correct answer: **B**

A. Incorrect. Cloud protocol simulators are a way to do network protocol compatibility testing.

B. Correct. Renting cloud-hosted agents is a way to simulate a large number of connecting devices.

C. Incorrect. Checking the emulator against real devices is a way to verify an emulator.

D. Incorrect. Generating load according to operational profiles is important whether the cloud is used or not.

Question 11 Correct answers **D and E**

A. Incorrect. Transaction data must also be used for functional testing.

B. Incorrect. GPS information must also be used for functional testing.

C. Incorrect. Images must also be used for functional testing.

D. Correct. Variations in load, such as activity bursts and other high levels of load, are typical of performance and reliability testing.

E. Correct. Variations in load, such as peak usage levels and other high levels of load, are typical of performance and reliability testing.

4.6 Test your knowledge

Question 12 Correct answer: **A**

A. Correct. As mentioned in option A, keyword-driven approaches are an example of traditional test automation techniques used for mobile application testing.

B. Incorrect. Test automation is actually quite important for mobile apps.

C. Incorrect. Server-side components are especially testable using traditional internet and client–server automation techniques.

D. Incorrect. Exploratory testing is a manual technique.

CHAPTER 5

5.1 Test your knowledge

Question 1 Correct answer: **D**

A. Incorrect. Mobile apps and mobile devices will both continue to increase, since, in spite of consolidation in the phone market, other mobile devices continue to appear.

B. Incorrect. Mobile apps and mobile devices will both continue to increase, since, in spite of consolidation in the phone market, other mobile devices continue to appear.

C. Incorrect. Mobile apps and mobile devices will both continue to increase, since, in spite of consolidation in the phone market, other mobile devices continue to appear and there are virtually no barriers to entry for new apps.

D. Correct. Mobile apps and mobile devices will both continue to increase, since, in spite of consolidation in the phone market, other mobile devices continue to appear and there are virtually no barriers to entry for new apps.

Question 2 Correct answer: **B**

A. Incorrect. People will expect a steady stream of new features and fixes, with high quality as well.
B. Correct. Expectations for speed of delivery and quality will increase, as has been the case for PC and internet apps.
C. Incorrect. User experience will continue to be a key to success for mobile apps.
D. Incorrect. The convenience of mobile usage, together with the ease of delivering mobile apps, will continue to drive growth.

5.2 Test your knowledge

Question 3 Correct answer: **A**

A. Correct. Time and resources will always be limited, so focus on what's important by using risk analysis.
B. Incorrect. While suitability, accuracy, interoperability, and security are important, so are performance, reliability and portability, so consider both functional and non-functional test automation.
C. Incorrect. While suitability, accuracy, interoperability, and security are important, so are performance, reliability and portability, so consider both functional and non-functional test automation.
D. Incorrect. Due to short life cycles and tight funding in many situations, automated tests must achieve a positive ROI more quickly.

Question 4 Correct answer: **D**

A. Incorrect. While you wouldn't purchase any iOS or other smartphone devices in this scenario, you shouldn't purchase all supported Android devices when you can rent them.
B. Incorrect. It's not always true that a tablet would have more resources than a phone and it's also the case that the screen layout is very different, which could cause issues.
C. Incorrect. Some of these devices might be quite expensive and yet available as data sources for free or very cheaply on the internet.
D. Correct. Exploiting cloud-based devices for most compatibility testing minimizes the number of devices that must be purchased and maintained.

5.3 Test your knowledge

Question 5 Correct answer: **C**

A. Incorrect. Waterfall is appropriate in some cases, but for many apps an incremental approach is better.
B. Incorrect. Lean methods such as Kanban are becoming more popular even now.
C. Correct. The waterfall-style "test bugs out at the end" approach won't work for fast-paced mobile app development.
D. Incorrect. Agile and Lean methods both involve testers throughout the process.

5.4 Test your knowledge

Question 6 Correct answer: **A**

A. Correct. Mobile app development is still a relatively young field, so it will change rapidly and you'll need to learn new skills as technologies evolve.
B. Incorrect. The rapid growth of the ISTQB® is proof that testing continues to grow as a profession.
C. Incorrect. Both functional and non-functional tests are important.
D. Incorrect. You should master existing tools, but be aware of new tools as they come out.

INDEX

Page numbers in italics refer to figures and tables

ISTQB Performance Tester syllabus 81

Juran, J.M. 31

Kanban development model 23, 143
keyword granularity 133
keyword-driven automation 131–4, 155
Kindles 6
Kruchten, Philippe 23

Lego 138
life cycle models 22–4, 143
load testing 80

Martin, James 23
McConnell, Steve 23
memory 107–8, 153
memory leaks 108
mobile applications 6–7
mobile devices 6
mobile-optimized websites 6–7, 113
Myers, Glenford 69

NASA 137
native applications 6, 16, 113
navigational applications *28*, 29
non-functional testing 79–96
notification-interruption testing 66

object-oriented software 142
open-source testing tools 102
OWASP (Open Web Application Security Project) 58–60

pairwise testing 69
Paloma Airlines website 60, *70*, *71*, 88–9, *90*

performance testing 80–6, 150
persona testing 72, 83, 87
portability testing 91–3
    testing tools 124–8
power consumption 66–7
PRAM (Pragmatic Risk Analysis and Management) technique 36
project risks 32
protocols 110, 152
purpose-built devices 6

quality risks 31–40

random access memory (RAM) 107
Rapid Application Development (RAD) model 23, 143
Rational Unified Process (RUP) development model 23, 143
RBCS 30, 58n
real world considerations 153
reliability testing 93–6
resource usage/utilization 80, 82
risk priority numbers 39, 40
risk-based testing 30–40, 48
Royce, Winston 23

safety 81
scalability testing 80
SD cards 64
security 43
security testing 55–6, 56–61
senior users 43–4, 45
server-side controls 59
server-side security 61
server-side testing tools 101
session handling 59
Simon Personal Communicator 1
simulators 92, 118–21
Six Sigma technique 142
SMS 57

software releases 13
Software Testing Techniques (Boris Beizer) 142
Spiral development model 23
stack memory 107–8
state-based testing 69
stress testing 80
suitability testing 55

test analysis 47
test conditions 47–50
Test Storming technique 74–7
testing tools 98–105, 152
thin/thick-client applications 16
throughput 80
tools
    see testing tools
Total Quality Management technique 142
traceability 40, 48

United Airlines website 7
untrusted inputs 59
usability testing 86–91, 150–1
use cases 69
user personas
    see persona testing
user perspectives/scenarios 72
users 7–11, 27

variability 63–4
video gaming 81–2

walled garden 65
Watson, Thomas 1
Whittaker, James 69

Yelp application 24

www.ingramcontent.com/pod-product-compliance
Lightning Source LLC
Chambersburg PA
CBHW060134060326
40690CB00018B/3869